Fundamentals of Strategic Planning in a Global Economy

R. Henry Migliore

President, Managing for Success Professor Emeritus NSU/UCT

Managing for Success

Tulsa, Oklahoma

Fundamentals of Strategic Planning in a Global Economy
978-0-9989006-2-9

Copyright © 2018 by R. Henry Migliore

Published by
Managing for Success
10839 S. Houston
Jenks, Oklahoma 74037
www.hmigliore.com

Printed in the United States of America.
All rights reserved under International Copyright Law.

Table of Contents

FOREWORD

Among the leading figures in the field who have made management by objectives (MBO) a practical system of management, Henry Migliore is distinguished by his innovative approach. Not only does he understand the fundamentals, which he stresses in his writing and consulting, but his agile mind and energetic approach press him into areas of application and practice that others could have discovered but did not. His work in blue-collar applications of MBO is still so far ahead of the field that he stands practically alone in that huge area of application. This grows out of his actual experience in the factory at Continental Can, a bias I share with him, having held a similar post with the competitor in that industry many years ago.

In the present work he has shown his breadth of view by seizing on the top-level applications of MBO in long-range and strategic planning. Considerable pressure exists on firms to sharpen strategic planning and the contribution of this book to that important area of concern is considerable. It enlarges the old applications of MBO to encompass multi-year plans and strategies, which are the major concerns of top management in today world of rapid change. The content is terse and fact-based, and it comprises a model for management that top management can expand upon to widen their MBO efforts to encompass a new and highly valuable area.

George S. Odiorne
Amherst, Massachusetts

Henry Migliore is once again a step ahead of his time. His work at Continental Can in the mid-sixties pioneered Blue Collar MBO. In the seventies, he simplified strategic planning. In the eighties he made innovative applications in a variety of not-for-profit settings. In the nine- ties he has pioneered a simplified approach to planning into books for churches, hospitals, non-profit higher education and athletes.

This book brings his very practical ideas and practices on strategic planning on line for application in the next century and beyond. It is unique because it covers in detail the development of planning in the four vital areas of production, marketing, finance, and human resources. The emphasis on teamwork among functional areas ties them all together in a way that is both creative and workable.

Finally, Migliore uses this book to introduce his Culture Index. His understanding of corporate cultures and its importance in organizational planning, management, and control systems provides, indeed, a twenty-first century perspective.

Dr. Roger Fritz

PREFACE

An ever-present problem with organizations is determining strategic direction, developing a plan, and then managing the plan. Small organizations, particularly those under one owner/manager/organizer, usually cope fairly easily in the early years. But growth, addiction of personnel, and expansion soon turn a one-time simple problem into one much more complex. Unless management keeps fully abreast, an organization can become sluggish and victimized by a loss of direction.

Large organizations can be drifting and have no real direction. They are often plagued by a lack of innovation and an inability to respond to problems and opportunities.

This book discusses a philosophy of management that has convincingly demonstrated its value in bringing order out of chaos. It compels the management team to agree to direction. It is simple to understand. Once in motion it acquires a natural rhythm. It offers the opportunity to satisfy higher-level needs. Finally, and highly important, it provides a foundation to manage the organization. It gets everyone involved in the planning process.

I have assisted in applying this management philosophy in large and small enterprises, including a railroad, a coal mine, a pipeline company, manufacturing companies, churches, athletic departments, hospitals, government units, medical practices, educational units, and personal lives. Results have invariably been gratifying. I sincerely hope that the book will help the reader plan and manage effectively.

In the 21st century there is a dual concern for survival and growth. The planning and management system outlined here can assist the organization in achieving both.

Organization of the Book

Chapter 1 sets the base for the introduction of my strategic planning and management system.

Chapters 2, 3, and 4 develop the actual long-range planning process. Here is where I introduce my own thinking. If the reader works his way through these chapters and fills in the appropriate, required information, they will have a rough draft of a strategic long-range plan. Chapters 5, 6, 7, 8, and 9 cover how to develop functional plans. Chapter 10 covers how to strategically manage the plans. Chapter 11 covers the appraisal and reward process. Chapter 12 discusses the Culture Index. Chapter 13 summarizes the Long-Range Planning/MBO and strategic management process.

ACKNOWLEDGMENTS

I would like to acknowledge the following persons for contributions and insights that helped me to develop this planning system: my professor at the University of Arkansas, Dr. Richard Johanson, and Dr. George Odiorne. Both provided me hours of review and discussion in arriving at the final product.

Persons who presented ideas and thoughts for me on the basis of a study of their work were Peter Drucker and Dale McConkey.

I would also like to acknowledge the many companies and organizations that I have worked with over the past 50 years. This interaction provided the learning opportunity through actual practice to develop the theories and concepts presented. Included in this are Studies I and II, in chapter seven that were presented at Southwest Business Symposium, College of Business, Central State University, April, 1988.

Chapter Five is adapted from an article coauthored with my longtime friend and associate, Dr. Robert E. Stevens.

Chapter Nine is adapted from a working paper developed with Dr. Steve Haines, La Jolla, California.

A special note of thanks goes to Linda Massey in the Business Center at Oral Roberts University.

The joy and balance provided by my wonderful family were a blessing. Finally, I thank God for the experience, skills, and insights given to me in order to write this book to serve others.

R. Henry Migliore

CHAPTER 1
INTRODUCTION: PLANNING PERSPECTIVES

*A well-defined mission serves as a constant reminder of the need
to look outside the organization not only for "customers"
but also for measures of success.*

Peter Drucker, Management Expert

What Is Strategic Planning?

The word tstrategic means, pertaining to strategy. Strategy is derived from the Greek word *strategos,* which means generalship, art of the general, or more broadly, leadership. The word "strategic" when used in the context of planning provides a perspective to planning, which is long-run in nature and deals with achieving specified end results. Just as military strategy has the objective of the winning of the war, so too, strategic planning has as its goal the achievement of the organization.

Strategic decisions must be differentiated from tactical decisions. Strategic decisions outline the overall game plan or approach, while tactical decisions involve implementing various activities, which are needed to carry out the larger strategy. For example, a company which decides to change locations because of shifting population trends and industrial development around the present location is making strategic decisions. Then many other decisions must be made about the exact location, size of building, parking facilities, and other major details. These all have long-term implications and are therefore strategic in nature.

Then other decisions such as wall colors, decor, communications and air conditioning must be made. These are tactical decisions needed to carry out or implement the strategic decision previously made. Thus, strategic decisions provide the overall framework within which the tactical decisions are made. It is critically important that leaders of all organizations be able to differentiate between these types of decisions to identify whether the choice has short-term or long-term implications.

The Strategic Planning Process

The strategic planning process is basically a matching process involving internal resources and its external opportunities. The objective of this process is to peer through the "strategic window" and identify opportunities the individual organization is equipped to take advantage of or respond to. Thus the strategic management process can be defined as *a managerial process which involves matching the organization capabilities with its opportunities.* These opportunities are identified over time, and decisions revolve around investing or divesting resources to address these opportunities. The context in which these strategic decisions are made is: (1) the firm's operating environment, (2) the firm's purpose or mission, and (3) the firm's organization-wide objectives. Strategic planning is the process, which ties all these elements together to facilitate strategic choices that are consistent with all three areas and then implements and evaluates these choices.

The successful results of planning described earlier can be achieved through implementing an effective strategic planning process. The following breakdown of this process is a complete outline of a system capable of creating true changes in a firm's attitudes as well as its productivity.

It is important to recognize at this point what we call "the two Ps." The first "P" means Product: get the plan in writing. The plan must be something you can hold in your hand, a written product of your efforts. If the plan is not in writing, it is called daydreaming. When it is in writing, you are telling yourself and others you are serious about it. The second "P" represents Process: every plan must have maximum input from everyone. Those who execute the plan must be involved in construction of the plan in order to gain their commitment. The best way to ensure a plan's failure is to overlook both the product and the process. They are equally important.

While there are many different ways in which a firm can approach the strategic planning process, a systematic approach that carries the organization through a series of integral steps helps focus attention on answering a basic set of questions each organization must answer:

1. *What will we do?* This question focuses attention on the specific needs the firm will try to meet in the marketplace.

2. *Who will we do it for?* This question addresses the need for the firm to identify the various market segments whose needs will be met.

3. *Why do our customers want to do business with our firm?*

4. *Why do our employees work for our company?*

5. *Who is our <u>real</u> competition?*

6. *How will we do what we want to do?* Answering this question forces thinking about the many avenues through which the firm's efforts may be channeled.

7. *How big should the firm be in the future? What is the optimum size?*

8. *What changes are taking place?*

Strategic Planning: A Definition

Strategic Planning and Management is a philosophy of managing based on identifying purpose, objectives, and desired results, and establishing a realistic program for obtaining these results and evaluating performance in achieving them.

The following nine-point breakdown of this process is productivity. This definition establishes a true strategic long-range planning and management system.

Such a philosophy involves:

1. Defining an organization's purpose and reason for being.

2. Monitoring the environment in which it operates.

3. Realistically assessing its strengths and weaknesses.

4. Making assumptions about unpredictable future events.

5. Prescribing written, specific, and measurable objectives in principal result areas contributing to the organization's purpose.

    a. Negotiating and bargaining at every level from top line and staff positions down to the blue-collar level.
    b. Recognizing a performance contract embracing the agreed-upon objectives.

6. Developing strategies on how to use available resources to meet objectives.

7. Making long- and short-range plans to meet objectives.

8. Constantly appraising performance to determine whether it is keeping pace with attainment of objectives and is consistent with its defined purpose.

    a. Being willing to change or modify objectives, strategies, and plans when conditions change
    b. Evaluating progress at every stage so that needed changes can be made smoothly.
    c. Making sure that rewards are thoughtfully considered and are appropriate for the accomplishment, recognizing the strengths and weaknesses of the extrinsic and intrinsic rewards.

9. Reevaluating purpose, environment, strengths, weaknesses, and assumptions before setting objectives for the next performance year.

This definition has been sent to dozens of academic, consulting, and business people for review and suggestions. Many shared in the final wording of the definition. Nearly all the respondents agreed that this definition advances the state of the art and better demonstrates that a planning and management system can be the center of managing the organization for survival, growth, and a more efficient organization.

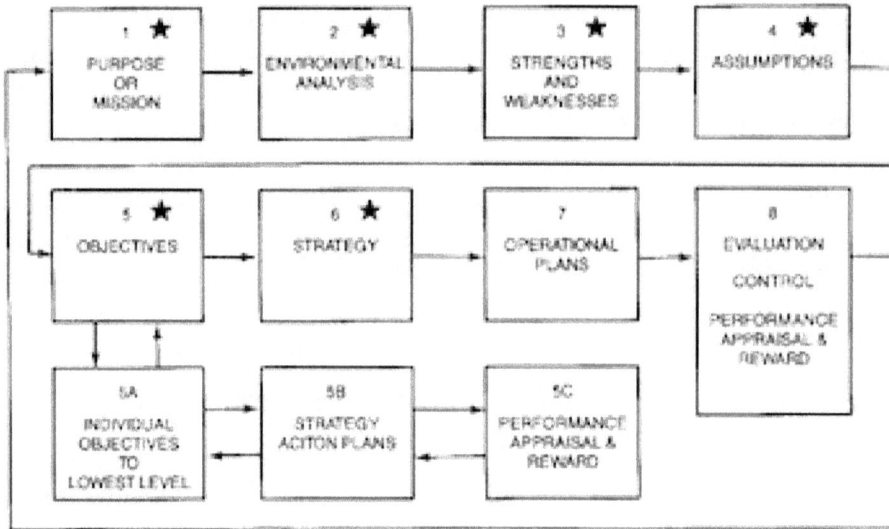

It is important to remember that the strategic planning process is as important as the product. The nine steps are important because of the questions the organization is forced to consider. Each step requires organization levels to discuss, study, and negotiate. This process develops a planning mentality. When the nine steps are complete, you do have a product: a strategic plan. Managing the strategic plan is a learned art. The longer you use the tool, the better you are able to manage it.

If an organization uses the nine-step Strategic Long-Range Planning process outline, it can count on the following benefits:

1. The organization will determine where it is going.

2. Opportunities and risks will be identified.

3. All organization members will be forced into a consensus as the direction for the organization is identified.

4. A surge of excitement will be experienced as managers have the opportunity to have input into the planning process.

5. Communication in all directions will be instantly improved.

6. Nonproductive persons will fall by the wayside.

7. Increases should be expected in all measurable areas—profitability, productivity, turnover, etc.

8. Within a year, a personal training and development plan will evolve for all persons in the organization.

Importance and Justification

The United States economy, and the capitalistic concept, must continue to be a system for the world to follow. A properly functioning planning system organizes men, money, and machines to be more effective and productive.

As we move into the new millennium, the economy is strong with low inflation and a low unemployment rate. Productivity is on the rise. The majority of employees are satisfied with their jobs yet experience more job insecurity due to the trend in downsizing, rightsizing, and re-engineering as companies struggle to be more competitive in an increasingly global business environment.

The Council of Economic Advisors reported in early 1999 that the country's longest peacetime expansion had occurred over the previous 93 months due to the economy's continued growth. The nation's unemployment rate is at a 29-year low at 4.2 percent. Productivity the last two quarters of 1998, at 4 percent and 4.3 percent respectively, was the best six-month performance since 1983. These productivity gains have been attributed to continued cost reduction strategies and extensive use of technology such as computers for increased efficiency (Laabs. 1999).

The "Working Trends" survey conducted by the John J. Heldrich Center for Workforce Development at Rutgers University and the Center for Survey Research and Analysis at the University of Connecticut revealed that 88 percent of employees surveyed were satisfied with their jobs and 54 percent considered themselves to be "very satisfied." However, 71 percent had concerns about job security (Hinden, 1999). A two-year study by a New York nonprofit research group, the Families and Work Institute, revealed that due to downsizing trends over the last five years, one third of employees felt "somewhat likely or very likely" they would be laid off within the next few years (Miller, 1999).

Downsizing has occurred in both the private and public sectors. According to the U.S. Bureau of Labor Statistics, over 3.3 million employees were laid off between 1996 and 1998. Between 1989 and 1998, there was a 33 percent reduction in the armed forces, impacting over 700,000 people (Scott, 1999). According to the Office of Personnel Management, over 200,000 civil service jobs were eliminated between 1993 and 1998 Joyner, 1998).

Companies are trying to learn to right size and respond quickly to continual changes in the marketplace. As employees in one part of a company are selectively being laid off, another area of the company may be hiring. Other factors impacting this rightsizing trend are mergers and acquisitions as well as rapid growth in technology. According to a 1998 American Management Association survey on downsizing, 41 percent eliminated jobs yet two-thirds of those were at the same time creating new jobs (Cavsey, 1999)..

Need for Strategic Planning

Not to be overlooked is the importance of planning to ensure the survival of the firm. With competition, new products and services, and an ever-changing complex world, a firm must have a system of managing that forces it to think through its alternative. A more detailed planning gap discussion is covered in Chapter 5.

What is needed is a management mentality to help organizations and managers survive as we enter the 21st century. We can no longer count on doing business the way we have in the past. I believe that of the existing American business organizations, one-third will fall by the wayside by the year 2010. The complexities in the marketplace, political arenas, and new product improvement will require organizations to adapt to changing situations. The Strategic Planning Process is the key tool in helping managers through the turbulent times ahead.

Any entity unable to adapt to changing times, whether it is dinosaurs, buggy whips, or whale oil, will not make it in the future. Organizations that did not adapt include the Penn Central Railroad, W.T. Grant, Pan American and Eastern Airlines, to mention a few.

I am sure that years ago their management teams would have scoffed at the idea they would no longer be in existence today. IBM, General Motors, and Sears adapted only after losing market share.

Peter F. Drucker makes an all-important point: "All institutions live and perform in two time periods: today and tomorrow. Tomorrow is being made today irrevocably in most cases" (Drucker, 1980). The key point Drucker is emphasizing is that today we are making decisions that will affect the organization in the future. The planning process outlined in this book will help to make those important, far-reaching decisions in a scientific and logical manner.

We are in an era that must emphasize long-range thinking. Dale O. Cloninger, in the article "American Myopia," believes that our very way of life has contributed toward a concern with only short-term results. He states, "As a whole Americans tend to be impatient, insisting on "instantness"— instant success, instant gratification, instant service, and instant satisfaction" (Cloninger, 1981).

I believe this mentality has permeated our management system. Cloninger also says, "What is reasonable is to expect a greater emphasis on long-term planning and a recognition of the importance of patience through the realization that care, planning, hard work, and progress towards longer term goals carry their own rewards." I believe we are in an era in which management systems must seek out and reward those managers who can skillfully guide organizations toward longer term purpose and objectives and with less emphasis on the short-term profitability and reward. This Strategic Planning Process, by its very nature, forces a forward-looking view.

A portion of this book addresses the planning problem. When I assumed the responsibility of long-range planning at Continental Can Company's Elwood plant, I realized that I was not to run a one-man show. For the program to work, I acknowledged that everyone had to be involved. I was fully aware of my limited knowledge about manufacturing, engineering, and traffic, all of which would have to be meshed into the planning program. For any plan to succeed it had to have the support of every phase of the operation, otherwise what would evolve would be my plan and not that of the whole organization. By having this kind of involvement in the planning process, all of the persons needed to assure successful decisions would have been involved in the process.

Richard P. Nielsen observes in a recent article, "When an institution decides to develop a strategic plan often it is important that key individuals and groups reach consensus on the decision." What is being emphasized here is the need for this consensus and discussion, so that once the plan is agreed upon the implementation will go quickly (Nielsen, 1981).

Our American management system generally makes fast decisions with only a few persons involved and then struggles for years and sometimes unsuccessfully gets the decisions implemented. The Japanese are one up on us in this area. They spend seemingly endless time analyzing the situation, studying the problem, looking at all avenues of the decision-making process before making a decision. Everyone has his/her say before the decision is made. Typically, they then move much faster in getting the decision implemented than we do in our American system. I believe the planning system discussed here brings out the best in our decision-making process. The need is to react quickly, bring people together so that consensus is made and decisions can be implemented quickly. How important is strategic planning? Robert Albanese of Texas A&M notes:

> One study of 58 business organizations with identifiable formal planning functions (not necessarily planning departments) found that the individuals responsible for formal planning spend half their time working alone, reading, and writing reports. The study suggests that the formal planner's relative isolation from meetings with managers and other organization members may be one factor contributing to a lack of planning effectiveness. The danger of such isolation can be reduced If planning is not separated from the implementation of plans (Albanese, 1970).

A study done in 1998 of 177 firms in the six-million-dollar revenue range in the Midwest confirmed the hypothesis. For firms, the higher the level of strategic planning in small business, the greater the level of firm performance. This suggests that the higher the level of perceived environmental uncertainty, the greater the level of strategic planning required.

The results presented provide support for hypothesis 4 ($p<0.05$). The regression results show that strategic planning has a positive association with performance when using Return of Assets (ROA) as dependent variable. This suggests that the higher the level of strategic planning committed by the small business, the higher the level of business performance (Matthews, 1999).

The planning system described here guards against the problems Albanese mentions. All management levels are involved and are responsible for executing the plan.

Sidney Schoeffler and co-authors found in a study of 57 corporations with 620 diverse businesses that there is a relationship between strategic planning and nonprofit performance. In his summary, he says that it has been demonstrated that strategic planning can have a positive impact on profits (Schoeffler, Buzzell, and Heaney, 1974).

Planning systems can cover a varied set of time frames. My wife, Mari, in her tenure as president of the Oral Roberts University Women's Club, had a planning horizon of one year. Once the plan was set, it became a process of execution, re-planning, and evaluation to finish the term of office. Planning for Colowyo Coal Company to mine its federal lease covers more than five years. Weyerhaeuser's corporation plans its tree crops for 20 to 40 years. The planning system described in this book can cover any time frame. It can be used by any individual, organization, business, (profit or nonprofit) or group.

Ronald J. Kudia reports in a study of the effect of strategic planning on the returns of stockholders that he found no significant differences between the shareholders of planning and non-planning firms. Other companies, including 3M and Bendix, attribute planning to superior performance. Kudia discusses a number of studies that indicates strategic planning resulted in positive effects (Kudia, 1980).

In a 1996 *Business Week* article, John A. Byrne observed that after 10 years of slashing and downsizing to remain competitive in the global marketplace, strategic planning is on the rise as organizations seek to improve the bottom line with their re-engineered and rightsized organizations. Strategic planning sessions include staff from all levels of the organization, not just those at the top; even customers and suppliers participate with each offering unique perspective. Byrne added that a study by the Association of Management Consulting Firms revealed that "executives, consultants and [business] school professors all agree that business strategy is now the single most important management issue and will remain so for the next five years." Byrne notes that with sound strategy "companies are pursuing novel ways to hatch new products, expand existing businesses and create the markets of tomorrow" (Byrne, 1996).

Peter Drucker asserts that there are seven management principles that are no longer valid in today's environment (Drucker, 1998). He notes the following as fallacies: "(1) there is only one right way to organize a business (2) the principles of management apply only to business organizations (3) there is a single right way to manage people."

Early management thinking theorized that the only way to organize operations was with functional departments managed separately with all reporting to the CEO at the top.

This centralization was followed by decentralization, and now the team concept in various forms is popular. Drucker emphasizes:

> "In any enterprise there is a need for a number of different organizational structures coexisting side by side." And says, "The executive of the future will need to be able to use each one properly, and to think in terms of mixed structures rather than pure structures." The management guru also makes the case that every organization, whether a business corporation, religious or charity organization, healthcare group, university, or government agency, needs to follow similar sound management principles in order to achieve success. He adds that the difference between these types of organizations "applies to only 10 percent of the work which is determined by the organization's specific mission, its culture, its history, and its vocabulary. The rest is pretty much interchangeable."

Drucker insists that just as there is no one right way to organize a business there is also not one single way to manage employees. He states his philosophy in the past had been consistent with Theory Y in that people want to work, and managers just need to motivate them. His thesis changed after reading *Eupsychian Management* by Abraham H. Maslow in 1962 in which Maslow demonstrated "conclusively that different people need to be motivated differently." Drucker notes most of today's employees are not true subordinates who are there just to do what they are told but are "knowledge workers." They can do their job better than the boss, and thus should be managed as associates. He adds that the same things that motivate volunteers motivate knowledge workers: "above all, challenge, the need to know the organization's mission and to believe in it, a need for continuous training, and a need to see results." Managers need to lead rather than "manage," and can help the organization by "aligning the employee's goals with those of the organization and vice versa."

The other management theories that were valid in the past and are now considered outdated by Drucker are: (1) That technologies, markets, and end users are fixed and rarely overlap. (2) That management's scope is legally defined as applying only to an organization's assets and employees.(3) That management's job is to "run the business" rather than to concentrate on what is happening outside the business, that is, management is internally, not externally, focused. (4) That national boundaries define the ecology of enterprise and management.

Drucker insists that one new assumption is that "the technologies likely to have the greatest impact on a company and its industry are technologies outside of its own field." One example highlighting this point was the development of the transistor by Bell Labs, part of AT&T. Thinking that the applications for this new invention were mainly outside the telephone industry, they sold it for a mere $25,000 to any company that was interested. These companies included Intel, Sony, and Compaq.

End users are not fixed. Markets change and companies need to adapt. Few businesses achieve greater than 30 percent market share, leaving 70 percent as potential customers if an organization can determine how to meet their needs.

Drucker notes that:

> "The rapid decline of the American department store in the 1970s and 1980s was not caused by their customers deserting them. The 30 percent of American housewives who were their customers remained loyal, but a new breed of educated working women did not adopt the department store habit. She didn't have the time. Since she was not a customer, the department stores paid little attention to her. By the time she became the biggest part of the affluent middle class, it was too late for the department store to win her loyalty. Instead, by catering to its regular customers, these retailers ended up catering to a dying breed."

Drucker also states that the scope of management needs to be refined to include the entire economic process where main suppliers are involved in joint planning, development, and design and both work as partners to create value. We are operating in an increasingly global environment. Drucker notes that companies have been operating internationally for some time. The difference is that in the past whole companies did business in a foreign country; now, different pieces of the business process are being produced in different countries, resulting in multinational products and a broader scope internationally.

A manager's principal job is not to run the organization but to innovate, Drucker insists. He asserts that "an enterprise, whether a business or any other institution, that does not innovate or does not engage in entrepreneurship will not long survive." He considers four entrepreneurial practices to be essential:

> "(1) the organized abandonment of products, services, processes, markets, distribution channels and so on that are no longer an optimal allocation of resources, (2) to organize for systematic, continuing improvement, (3) to organize for systematic and continuous exploitation, especially of ... successes, (4) to organize systematic innovation, that is, to create the different tomorrow that makes yesterday obsolete, and to a large extent, replaces even the most successful products of today in any organization."

Strategic Management

Strategic Management is a philosophy of managing with a planning process. It is a stream of decisions and actions, which effectively execute the strategic plan. The strategic management process is the way the management team directs the organization within the framework and promotion of the strategic plan.

Strategic decisions are a means to achieve ends. These decisions encompass the definition of the business, products and markets to be served, functions to be performed, and major policies needed for the organization to execute these decisions to achieve objectives. Strategic management provides a strong incentive for employees and management to achieve company objectives. It serves as the basis for management control and evaluation. It allows a firm to innovate in time to take advantage of new opportunities in the environment and reduce its risk because it anticipated the future. Strategic management is a continuous process.

The importance of strategic management became apparent when many organizations developed plans and then put them on the shelf. The yearly planning process would be completed, and the organization went back to its old way of doing things. Strategic management evolved because of the need to manage the plan.

Long-range planning helps remove some of the risks and ambiguity associated with organizational memberships. Strategic management allows an enterprise to base its decisions on long-range forecasts, not spur-of-the-moment reactions. It allows the firm to take action at an early stage of a new trend and consider the lead-time for effective management. This helps ensure full exploitation of opportunities.

Strategic management allows a firm's top executives to anticipate change and provides direction and control for the enterprise, while it allows them to have unified opinion on strategic issues and actions. It also helps educate managers to become better decision-makers. It helps them examine basic problems of a company. It improves corporate communication, the coordination of individual projects, the allocation of resources, and short-range planning such as budgeting. Strategic management focuses on business problems, not just functional problems such as those of a marketing or financial nature.

Strategic management focuses on "second-generation planning," analysis of the business, and the preparation of several scenarios for the future.

This is not to say that strategic management is all you need to make a success of your business, but it should prove to be informative. A good example of both strategic planning and strategic management is at Ford Motor Company. The management style of retired Ford Motor Company's Donald Petersen will be a model for chief executives for years to come. Ford's U.S. market share climbed in the 1980s to about 22 percent from 16 percent. Some of Petersen's handiwork was unique to Ford. He broke the habit of following GM's lead. Here are Petersen's lessons, and how they are applied.

1.   Be obsessed with quality. Petersen hired the late W. Edwards Deming, a quality master who taught the Japanese the secrets of statistical process control.

2.   Empower your workers. Petersen tapped into the creative power of every Ford worker.

3.   Tap the power of teams. Petersen forced the people who design cars to work in close-knit teams with Ford's engineers and marketers.

4.   Compete globally. Petersen turned Ford into the USA's first truly global automotive company (Hillkink, 1999).

Included in the area of strategic management is management responsibility to create a positive, productive work environment. A 1998 Fortune survey of most admired companies conducted by the Hay Group revealed that "the single best predictor of overall excellence was a company's ability to attract, motivate, and retain talented people" (*Fortune*, 1998). The corporate culture of those companies was crucial in the achievement of this goal according to their company's leaders. Bruce Pfau, a VP of the Hay Group and an expert in cultural assessment, notes that "the corporate cultures of high performing companies are dramatically different from those of average companies." Average company goals were "minimizing risk, respecting the chain of command, supporting the boss, and making budget" while high-performing companies valued "teamwork, customer focus, fair treatment of employees, initiative and motivation." The survey emphasizes that companies in the lead for their industry such as Southwest Airlines, Squibb, Toyota, JP Morgan, UPS, Intel, Dow Chemical, have top leadership that places high priority on cultural issues and knows how they measure up in comparison to those goals.

What is Planning?

Planning may be defined as a managerial activity that involves determining your fundamental purpose as an organization, analyzing the environment, setting objectives, deciding on specific actions needed to reach the objectives, and then adapting the original plan as feedback on results is received. This process should be distinguished from the plan itself, which is a written document containing the results of the planning process. The plan is a written statement of what is to be done and how it is to be done. Planning is a continuous process that both precedes and follows other functions. Plans are made and executed, and results are used to make new plans as the process continues.

Types of Plans

There are many types of plans, but most can be categorized as either *strategic* or *tactical.* Strategic plans cover a long period of time and may be referred to as *long-term.* They are broad in scope and basically answer the question of how an organization is to commit its resources over the next three to five, possibly even 10 years. Strategic plans are altered on an infrequent basis to reflect changes in the environment or overall direction of the organization.

Tactical plans cover a short time period, usually a year or less. They are often referred to as *short-term or operational plans.* They specify what is to be done in a given year to move the organization toward its long-term objectives. In other words, what we do this year (short-term) needs to be tied to where we want to be five to 10 years in the future (long-term).

Traditionally, managers who have been involved in planning have focused on short-term rather than long-term planning. This is better than no planning at all, but it also means each year's plan is not related to anything long-term in nature and usually falls short of moving the organization to where it wants to be in the future. Programs and events also require planning. A *program* is a large set of activities involving a specific area of capabilities, such as planning for a new outpatient surgery service or a new managed care system. Planning for programs involves:

1. Dividing the total set of activities into meaningful parts.

2. Assigning planning responsibility for each part to appropriate people.

3. Assigning target dates for completion of plans.

4. Determining and allocating the resources needed for each part, in other word, each major program or division within an organization should have a strategic plan in place to provide a blueprint for the program over time.

An *event* is generally a project of less scope and complexity. It is also not likely to be repeated on a regular basis. An event may be a part of a broader program, such as the grand opening of a new service, or it may be self-contained, such as an annual recruiting fair at the local mall. Even for a onetime event, planning is an essential element to accomplish the objectives of the project and coordinate the activities that make up the event.

The Greatest Needs of Today's Organizations Worldwide

In informal surveys I have made over the years, leaders of organizations appear strong in their beliefs that strategic planning is important. Yet simple acknowledgment of its importance is not enough for success. To put matters into perspective, let us try to translate success and better understand what makes the organization successful.

$$X = f (A, B, C, D, E, F, G, H, I \ldots)$$

In this case X represents success, a dependent variable, and is on the left side of the equation. The = sign means a balance, or equal to what is on the other side. The "f" means "a function of," indicating on what that success depends. On the right side are all the independent variables that affect success:

A.   Chief Executive as Leader/Manager/Planner

B.   Management Team Working Together

C.   Planning System

D.   Organizational Structure

E.   Control System

F.   Reward System

G.   Integrity/Ethics of Organization

H.   Empowered Employer

I.   Etc.

Only a few independent variables are listed, but the possibilities are endless. Notice that success is not necessarily equated with size. We are defining success in broader terms than number of employees, budget, and so forth. There seems to be a widespread notion that size is the only barometer of success, but we do not subscribe to that belief.

Untapped leadership exists in many organizations. I believe the greatest problems holding back these leaders and the organizations they serve involve some combination of independent variables C, D, and E. Management, planning, organization, and control are some of the greatest needs of all organizations.

Most people assume that all administrators are leaders to some degree, or they could not remain in their executive positions. However, their leadership efforts and the success of their organizations are in direct proportion to variables C, D, and E. If you assume all other variables remain unchanged and full effort goes into C, D, and E, then the X factor (success), the dependent variable, has to increase. Without training and knowledge in the area of planning and management, your chief executive places a ceiling on success. No organization can get any bigger than the capacity of its managers to manage. The hindrance is not the needs of the constituents, because the needs are always there.

If every executive could improve each of these areas just a little each year, they would be much more successful. They could reduce drastically all the obvious errors in direction, false starts, dissipated efforts, staff frustration, and waste. They could also successfully challenge a world rife with criticism about waste and inefficiency in organizations.

Organizations cannot afford to wait until someone comes along and stirs up a big scandal. We need to put our shoulders to the wheel and pay attention to management, planning, organization, control, and people. If we do not, on the whole, many of our organizations will not accomplish nearly as much as they might.

My observation is that many people in leadership positions are reluctant to plan, do not want a plan in writing, and do not ask for advice. The tendency is to be led by intuition, which is sometimes based on a whim or emotional impulse. This reflects our general American inclination to hang loose. Probably 75 percent of the organizations the author has observed or worked with have the same problem. Yet the 25 percent who have the discipline to plan and manage properly, far outperform those that do not. Higher revenue surpluses, better service and lower turnovers are but a few of the rewards of thoughtful, well-executed planning. Good fortune comes to those organizations that have the discipline to plan and manage effectively.

Many times there is the tendency to say that forces outside our control caused a plan or project to go sour. And sometimes that is the case. But too often we are our own worst enemies, holding ourselves back. Many business failures can be traced to poor planning, failure to get people involved in the planning and generally poor management.

Even where planning is done, we often sense a spirit of extreme urgency. Here the atmosphere is permeated with a "let's go for it, if it is a worthwhile service, it will prosper" mentality. What is the rush? Many HCOs need to slow down and plan. Often they have rushed around in circles for several years. If the organization provides a worthwhile service, it deserves our best efforts at careful planning. Included in doing our best is using the best planning and management philosophies and techniques available.

Fundamental to these efforts is effective goal setting. Its importance is to provide direction and unity of purpose. Where planning in organization occurs without quantitative goals clearly understood and widely supported, vigorous progress is unlikely and probably impossible. Planning is not easy, but the alternative is to be tossed to and fro, buffeted by every unforeseen circumstance, and blown off course.

And on a personal level, every leader needs a vision or a dream. Mission statements and dreams are the vessels through which personal desires can be fulfilled. Yet without specific goals, a vision is no vision.

In a society where many institutions are becoming stagnant, it is imperative that firms have an expanding vision. Thus, we see creative planning as the organization's best hope for a successful future. Solid purpose, long-range dreaming, and visionary thinking should be basic to a firm's operation. Too often planning in an organization has been met with little enthusiasm. Even in larger organizations, the enthusiasm for a plan seldom extends beyond a year unless it involves something tangible, such as a new building. Yet no matter how misunderstood and poorly appreciated planning is, it is a major factor in effective organization performance. The time for strategic planning in all organizations is *now*.

Planning Perspective

All organizations do at least some planning even if it is largely informal and even largely unintentional. One writer states, "planning has to be defined by the *process* it represents" (Drucker, 1974). The process is largely informal in many institutions which means it is also incremental (each decision builds upon prior planning decisions). Informal planning, however, leads to misunderstandings because there are few records of planning decisions which have been made, planning efforts are sporadic, and it is likely that the effort will not result in a completed plan. There is also no system of follow-through. Informal planning is not likely to be comprehensively implemented. Effective planning is a disciplined process.

If we have authority and responsibility in an organization, we find ourselves observing how the present is evolving into the future and how things we would like to see happen are sometimes (and sometimes not) becoming a part of that future. The extent to which we think about such things is the extent to which we are beginning the planning process. Planning begins with (1) the assumption that there is a future, and that (2) maybe it should be different than the present, along with (3) realizing that we can do something about that future, and then (4) resolving that we will take action.

Let us look at these four concepts. All of us know that there is a future. Not all of us care about the future. Most of us know that it will be at least a little different from the present even if we do nothing to bring about the difference. Many of us are content to have the fascinating future be created by others and are willing to sit back and take in the benefits of what that future might bring. Part of this is due to the expectation that the future will be better than the present. We point to the progress of this century. If we are from the United States or Canada, we look at how inventions, the standard of living, health care, and other improvements have come about without much effort on our part. Why mess up a good thing? If we continue as we have for the past 40 years and continue to avoid a major war, we expect prosperity, stability, convenience, better health, more wealth, and most other things that we value. In short, why plan when the world is getting better every day without planning effort on our part?

The second concept is determining whether we want the future to be different from the present and the past. Some of us say why bother? Some of us, on the other hand, find the future possibilities exciting. We consider ways in which the future will be different due to major forces such as the increased role of technology and technological breakthroughs, or the opportunities we face due to a strong economy and political freedom that encourage entrepreneurial and creative activities on our part and which work toward fulfilling our urges and interests.

The third concept is realizing that we can do something about that future. This requires vision, the ability to dream, to visualize what could happen if the right efforts take place. It begins with an understanding that the future can be different from the present, that you and others around you can help shape that future. It must include the understanding that the present is going to change anyway. The rapid rate of change in society today affects every aspect of an organization's life.

And then we have the fourth concept, resolving that we will take action to mold that future. This is the tough one. This means taking action based upon our vision of what we would like the future to be. The number of people who are serious in this category on a consistent basis is relatively small. The need for positive people in this category is very high. They are the ones who shape the world. These are the people who lead the world and create the interesting setting in which the rest of us live. The greatest opportunity is that each of us can decide whether we want to be in this category. There are no elections, no dues to pay, just leadership to exert and the satisfaction that comes from seeing something happen that has come about because of our leadership and the leadership of others.

Strategic Thinking

Strategic thinking is akin to critical thinking, a familiar concept in management theory. Traditionally, critical thinking has been identified with the field of logic and the mental ability to reason in the abstract. Today, critical thinking is an essential element of most disciplines including management, leadership, and strategic planning. Strategic thinking might be explained as focusing on higher-level learning and more complex thinking abilities. Thus, categories in the cognitive domain such as analysis, synthesis, and evaluation are rich fields for critical thinking. However, the focus is that of strategic planning in a practical and applied context. Therefore, we must direct critical thinking beyond knowledge within a discipline to application:

- Between disciplines
- To real-world predictable problems
- To real-world unpredictable problems

Strategic thinking also emphasizes:

- Asking and seeking answers to penetrating questions, which affect survival of the organization
- Scanning the environment, both external and internal, for unique ways of "doing more with less at higher quality"

A leader who thinks strategically will focus on the following:

- Conceptualize direction-setting actions for the organization
- Identify areas of change that will impact the vision, mission, and overall objective of the firm
- Look at the big picture across traditional boundaries and beyond the next two to three years
- Emphasize the why and the how (instead of what) of strategy design and implementation
- Search for the best competitive advantage, or best competitive position relative to other key institutions, which may target similar markets and donors.

Strategic thinking emphasizes development and implementation of organization-wide or overall strategies with accountability toward effectiveness, efficiency, and quality in mind. Perspectives of strategic thinking can be illustrated with the question, "Who are the two most important persons responsible for the success of an airplane's flight?" Typical responses would be:

- The pilot and the navigator.
- The pilot and the maintenance supervisor.
- The pilot and the air traffic controller.
- The pilot and the flight engineer.

All of these responses recognize the day-to-day hands-on importance of the pilot. They all introduce one of several other important support or auxiliary functionaries to the answer. However, each of these responses ignores the one person who is perhaps the single most important individual to the ultimate success of the airplane—the designer. Perhaps the pilot and the designer are the two individuals most important to the success of an airplane's flight because of the pilot's day-to-day responsibilities in commanding the craft and the designer's ability to create a concept that can be economically constructed, easily operated by any normally competent flight crew, and safely maintained by the ground crew.

Most contemporary administrators of organizations perceive themselves as the "pilots" of their institutions taking off, landing, conferring with the navigator, and communicating with the air traffic controller. They generally view themselves as the chief hands-on operational managers. However, what has been most lacking in these institutions in the past few years has been an appreciation for the strategic planning viewpoint. There is a need for more emphasis on an integrated "designer-pilot" approach to operating an education venture. A well-conceived, continuously updated strategic planning system can facilitate this emphasis.

An organization without a strategic planning perspective faces a tough situation. Instead of moving steadily toward its goals, the institution will continually swerve off course due to the endless supply of distractions that can prevent an institution from pursuing its vision and mission. Thus, strategic planning is one of the keys to success of any undertaking, and nowhere is it more important than in all organizations.

Ethics, Integrity, and Religious Principles in Business

Drucker's quote "the ultimate test of management is integrity" caught my attention in 1974 with the publication of his book, *Management: Tasks and Practices* (Drucker, 1974). At the time, I thought, no way. What about profits, market share, and customer service? By the early 80s, I began to understand what he was saying. Now as we enter the 21st century I agree 100 percent. Oral Roberts, then president of Oral Roberts University, spoke at a business seminar on the ORU campus. In his opening remarks he said, "Your product better be better than your sales pitch." In a brilliant, spirit-led speech before bankers from 38 states Roberts went on to relate the similarity between his product, ORU, and students raised to hear His voice, and products and services sold by the banks. As we look at promotions and deals by a wide range of organizations, it appears to me we are full circle back to "buyer beware." More and more there is "fine print," a hidden agenda.

How do we define integrity, ethics, and character? The dictionary gives us "firm attachment to moral or artistic principle: honesty and sincerity."

How are our society and business organizations measuring up to this definition? Some would say the trend is disturbing. The nation's CEO is still in office. His behavior would have resulted here in Tulsa with immediate removal from office. Our society does not seem to care. Many people went to prison over the savings and loan scandal. An international insurance company with questionable sales practices is refunding premiums. Instead of immediate refunds, they set up a cumbersome bureaucracy for the refund. The administration of the claim process problem amounts to more than the claim. Right after, we see ads on TV to "trust" this company. Another corporate giant admits to breaking the law collecting from customers. "That is big business!!"

Some would say, "Not here in Tulsa!" How about a 50 percent off coupon that a local company used recently? Upon investigation, the company almost doubled the original price and honored the 50 percent offer. This resulted in a real saving to the customer of only 10 percent instead of the advertised 50 percent. Good business practice? Short term, maybe. But what about the long term? These customers might not be back.

Peter Drucker said, "The ultimate test of management is integrity" in his 1974 look at management. I thought: "Come on profits and market share, return on investment? Any principled person could not argue against integrity, but management's "ultimate test"?

Twenty-five years later, I submit Drucker hit it on the head. Lawyers, laws, and court systems are not going to help you get a fair deal. My suggestion is deal only with organizations and people you can trust. Trust is gained over time. The issue is not what you say, as much as what you do.

My father, the late Roscoe Channing Migliore, taught me an early lesson in life. He was a merchant in Collinsville. Briefly, a freezer was delivered to a farmer on the verge of losing a freezer full of meat. Mr. Migliore, a union electrician, noticed the problem was in the electric cord. He fixed it in minutes. In the short run, he lost a sale. But, in the long run, his action confirmed what everyone in the Collinsville area already knew. You could trust Roscoe. Many, many years later he and the farmer by chance were in a nursing home together. Forty years later they were still discussing the incident.

I submit that integrity, ethics, and character are traits that are not only morally correct, but gain a trust that makes people want to do business with your organization.

Seven privately held companies that I have had close dealings with operate in an ethical way with a high degree of integrity. All seven companies are founded on Christian principles. They are: The Oklahoman Eagle, Parker Drilling, and T.D. Williamson, Inc., Tulsa, OK; Cross Manufacturing, Overland Park, KS; Michael Cardone Industries, Philadelphia, PA; and Brasfield Construction, Jackson, TN; and Aftermarket, Phoenix, Arizona. Except for Parker Drilling, I have been a consultant to the other six for many years. I am familiar with Parker Drilling because they are here in Tulsa, OK.

Many of my students work for Parker Drilling as do many of our friends. I am privileged to count Bobby Parker, Chairman of the Board, as a friend. I have been in countless strategy and operational meetings with the six companies mentioned. Each CEO has conferred with me on numerous decisions. Not once has any decision or action not met the highest standard of conduct. I count it as a privilege to have worked with and count these people as close friends.

Competitive Advantage

Competitive Advantage in the rapidly changing, fiercely competitive marketplace can be gained when the firm uses good planning and management principles. Michael E. Porter has made a significant contribution to the understanding of competitive advantage. His books *Competitive Strategy* and *Competitive Advantage* go into great detail on how to gain and maintain the competitive edge (Porter, 1980). He states:

> "Competition is at the core of the success or failure of firms. Competition determines the appropriateness of a firm's activities that can contribute to its performance, such as innovations, a cohesive culture, or good implementation. Competitive strategy is the search for a favorable competitive position in an industry, the fundamental arena in which competition occurs. Competitive strategy aims to establish a profitable and sustainable position against the forces that determine industry competition.

I submit that the firm that understands is committed and has the discipline to use the concepts in this book, and will gain a competitive edge.

Summary

I have attempted to establish in this chapter the belief that:

1. The demands of a volatile environment create an urgency for the planning concept.

2. Many of the identifiable organization failures cannot be blamed solely on unforeseen and uncontrollable factors, yet

3. Many leaders do not believe that there is a need for planning, but

4. There is a crucial place for better planning and management.

5. New planning creates opportunities and helps eliminate failures and lastly,

6. The firm gains a competitive advantage using the principles in the book.

The philosophy of this book is that in order for everyone in an organization—the board, the executive staff, the employees—to be successful, a strategic plan is desperately needed. If you look at the mistakes of the past, it is obvious that many organizations have floundered because they lack strategic direction. Over years of consulting with these types of organizations, the authors have observed this exact pattern in a large number of them. However, if you take the time and effort to study this book, the format prescribed here, and follow up with your people, this is what I believe you can expect:

1. A sense of enthusiasm in your organization.

2. A five-year plan in writing to which everyone is committed.

3. A sense of commitment by the entire organization to its overall direction.

4. Clear job duties and responsibilities.

5. Time for the leaders to do what they need to do.

6. Clear and evident improvement in the health and vitality of every member of the organization's staff.

7. Accountability, responsibility, delegation moving down, and lower organization ratios.

8. Rewarding results and behavior that are important to the firm and to the benefit of organization members.

9. Measurable improvement in the personal lives of all those in management positions with time for vacations, family, and personal pursuits.

Important Points to Remember

1. A workable Strategic Long-Range Planning/MBO program should include a specific pre-objective setting procedure.

2. We have a productivity problem in this country.

3. Long-range planning is essential to survival.

4. A general state of apathy and dissatisfaction exists at lower levels of the work force.

5. Problems have arisen with MBO when it is not used properly.

6. Many companies worldwide have had successful experiences with MBO.

7. There is scientific evidence of the merit of Long-Range Planning/MBO.

8. It is management's responsibility to provide the leadership to solve the productivity and planning problem.

9. There is a need for a simple, easy-to-understand, long-range planning tool.

10. The strategic plan must be strategically and systematically managed.

If you are struggling with any of the following problems or questions, this book may be very important to you:

- Why is there so much confusion among our vice presidents and department heads about what we are trying to accomplish?
- Why is there so much dissension and disagreement in this organization?
- Why is there such a high turnover of people in our organization, especially in leadership positions?
- Why did we spend money on new services when they are not being used?
- As CEO (Chief Executive Officer) why am I working 12 hours a day, and can never keep up?
- Why have we been less than successful on a number of projects and programs?
- Why have our revenues dropped off?
- Why does this organization lack enthusiasm?
- Why has the board asked me to resign after everything I have put into this organization?

If you are wrestling with any of these questions, the answer might be that your organization lacks effective long-term strategic planning and management.

References

Albanese, Robert. *Managing: Toward Accountability for Performance*. Cambridge, Mass.: Harvard University, 1970: 108-109.

Byrne, John. *Business Week*. 26 Aug. 1996: 26-51.

————."Managements New Paradigms" *Forbes*, 6 Oct. 199: 152.

Cavsey, Mike. "Downsizing Hits Home." *The Washington Post*, March 1, 1999.

Cloninger, Dale O. *The Collegiate Forum*, 1981.

Drucker, Peter. "Managing for Tomorrow." *Industry Week,* April 14, 1980: 55.

Drucker, Peter. . *Management: Tasks and Practices*. New York: Harper & Row, 1974.

Fortune "What Makes a Company Grow?" 26 Oct. 1998: 210

Greiner, Larry E. "Integrating Formal Planning into Organizations," in F.J. Aguilar, R.A. Howell, and R.F. Vancil, eds., Formal Planning Systems, 1970 (Cambridge, Mass.: Harvard University, Graduate School of Business Administration, 1970), p. 88.

Hillkink, John, "Peterson's Style Is a Model for the 1990s," *USA Today,* 1 March 1999: 813.

Hinden, Stan, "Forced to Retire Before You're Ready: The Merge and Downsize IRA's layoffs Hit Older Workers Especially Hard," *The Washington Post,* 6 June 1999.

Joyner, Tammy, "Massive Study Finds Workers Tired, Insecure," *The Atlanta Constitution,* 15 April 1998.

Kudl, Ronald J., "The Effects of Strategic Planning on Common Stock Returns," *Academy of Management Journal*, Vol. 23, No. 1:5, 1980.K

Laabs, Jennifer, "Has Downsizing Missed Its Mark?" *Workforce*, 1999.

Matthews, Charles H., Choy, Hoon Lee, "Antecedents and Consequence of Strategic Planning in Small Business: An Empirical Study." Naples, Italy, 23 June 1999.

Miller, Rich, "Worker Output up 4%; Productivity Bodes Well for Economy," *USA Today,* 12 May 1999.

Nielsen, Richard, "Toward a Method for Building Consensus During Strategic Planning," *Sloan Management Review,* 1981: 29.

Porter, Michael E., *Competitive Strategy*, The Free Press, 1980.

Porter, Michael E., *Competitive Advantage*, The Free Press, 1980.

Schoffler, Sidney, Robert D. Buzzell, and Donald F. Heaney, "Impact of Strategic Planning on Profit Performance," *Harvard Business Review,* March-April 1974: 137.

Shepard, Scott, "Workers Say Job Steals Family Time," *The Atlanta Constitution,* 18 March 1999.

Chapter 2
Purpose, Environmental Analysis, Strengths, and Weaknesses

Management's job is not to see the company as it is,
but as it can become.

John W. Teets CEO, Greyhound Corp.

This chapter will present discussion of the first three steps in the strategic planning process: on the mission and purpose of an organization, the environmental analysis, and how to assess strengths and weaknesses of the organization. The reader should be able to explain why these three steps must be completed before anything else is undertaken.

Further, the reader will be expected to be able to give an example of a purpose, an example of environmental analysis, and an example of strengths and weaknesses.

Purpose

The first and likely most important consideration when developing a long-range plan with this definition of SLRP/MBO is to define the purpose of or the "reason for being" for the organization of any specific part of it. This is usually a difficult process. Peter Drucker was the key influence in my logic to put this step first. I believe I never fully realized the importance of this until 1974, when Drucker's book came out. Oral Roberts is another that emphasized the purpose and mission of ORU. Drucker, in his book, *Management—Tasks, Responsibility and Practices*, defines the purpose of an organization. Here he starts with the marketing concept, which says to organize a business to satisfy a need in the marketplace. Drucker says, "It is defined by the want the customer satisfies when he buys a product or a service. To satisfy the customer is the mission and purpose of every business (Drucker, 1974). He continues, "Business enterprise, however, requires that the theory of the business be thought through and spelled out. It demands a clear definition of business purpose and business mission. It demands asking, 'What is our business and shat should it be (Drucker, 1974).

The purpose statement defined here encompasses the missions, dream and vision for the organization. It defines the reason for being, identifies needs in the marketplace. The scope of the operation, declares ethical and moral responsibility. It makes clear what business the organization is in.

The organization members must be continually reminded of the "reason for being."

Drucker stoutly declares,

> "Only a clear definition of the mission and purpose of the business makes possible clear and realistic business objectives. It is the foundation for priorities, strategies, plans, and working assignments. It is the starting point for the design of managerial jobs and, above all, for the design of managerial structures" (Drucker, 1974).

He continues,

> "Clearly, if purpose is defined casually or introspectively, or the list of key result areas neglects some of the less obvious threats and opportunities, the fabric of organization objectives and resources rests on shaky foundations. As Calvin Coolidge puts it: 'No enterprise can exist for itself alone. It ministers to some great need, it performs some great service not for itself but for others; or failing therein it ceases to be profitable and ceases to exist (Humble, 1969).

When I was dean of a College of Business, at the beginning of our planning sessions the administration and faculty of the School of Business defined, reviewed, and discussed our purpose statement. This practice kept us aware of and in tune with the world about us. Every business, organization, family, or person must have a clearly defined purpose. Note the purpose statement for **M. Cardone Industries** and **Trammell Crow**.

M. Cardone Industries

Statement of Purpose

M. CARDONE INDUSTRIES is a business enterprise. As a business, we realize a profit by meeting the needs of people. Profit permits expansion and strengthening of the business for the benefit of its owners, employees, customers and community. To this end, we pledge ourselves to:

1. Honor God in all we do

2. Help people develop

3. Pursue excellence

4. Grow profitably

Our business is the Remanufacturing of Automotive Products. Our market is the Automotive Aftermarket. Our purpose is to:

1. Provide the automotive after-market with products of the highest quality, a 100 percent order-fill, and the most responsive, efficient service available in the industry.

2. Contribute to the conservation of America's natural energy and mineral resources through our recycling of automotive parts.

3. Continually seek ways to offer our customers the greatest potential for profit.

We are an equal opportunity employer seeking to provide for our employees a safe, healthy, comfortable working environment. We encourage a holistic family atmosphere in our working relationships and seek to foster the belief that everyone at M. Cardone Industries is a vital part of a unified, precision team.

M. Cardone Industries is committed to conducting its business relationships in such a manner as to be a credit to God, its owners, our employees, their families, our customers, and the community. Each, though a separate entity, is part of a unified family and the mutual benefit of the whole is achieved as the needs of one another are considered.

Our position is that of a pioneer and proud leader in the automotive remanufacturing industry. We constantly pursue excellence and believe that:

If you want a long and satisfying life, never forget to be truthful and kind. If you want favor with both God and man, and a reputation for good judgment and common sense, then trust the Lord completely ... In everything you do, put God first, and He will direct you and crown your efforts with success."—Selections from the Bible: Proverbs 3: The Living Bible

Trammell Crow Company Philosophy

Serving Our Customer

As a marketing company, we have a preeminent commitment to serving the needs of our present and prospective tenants by developing buildings of the highest quality and providing superior building management and other services.

Our Valuable Relationships

We strive to nurture and expand mutually successful relationships with financing, construction, brokerage, and design, as well as other firms with whom we have the privilege of doing business. We are committed to creating and managing real estate properties for our lenders and investors that meet or exceed their investment objectives and to providing prompt, thorough, and accurate reporting on the performance of the investments.

Our Business Family

We are a company owned by our people. Because we believe our people are our greatest asset, we choose not to conduct ourselves as a large, impersonal company, but rather to operate as a business family with stewardship responsibilities to one another. Our company has been built around the dignity and worth of the individual and the recognition of personal achievement. We encourage full development of the talents of all our people, and are committed to reward and promote on the basis of merit. We manifest our pride in our people by providing each individual a personal stake in profitability of our business. We want our people to enjoy their work and we encourage a balance between work responsibilities, family life and community involvement

Profitability

By providing excellent service to our customers, by enhancing our outside relationships and by fostering the well-being of our people, we will generate cash flow, profits, and equity appreciation to capitalize our growth and achieve our other objectives.

In our business we believe in
- Individual entrepreneurship with local office autonomy
- Informal, consensus style of management
- Growth through shared experiences and mutual support
- Long-term ownership of assets
- Opportunities for management and ownership to those who distinguish themselves
- High quality, cost effective central services provided by a lean staff
- Honesty, integrity, excellence, hard work and fun

We are an evergreen company; we believe our prosperity in the future depends on our doing the right things today. With confidence in the future and in each other, yet with humility born of experiencing the cyclical nature and the risks inherent in our business, we strive for excellence, hoping to do the best job we can do and become the best people we can be.

Defining purpose is not always easy. Drucker describes how American Telephone & Telegraph Company defined its business purpose as:

> Our business is service. This sounds obvious once it has been said, But first there had to be the realization that a telephone system, being a natural monopoly, was susceptible to nationalization and that a privately owned telephone service in a developed and industrialized country was exceptional and needed community support for its survival. Second, there had to be the realization that community support could not be obtained by propaganda campaigns or by attacking critics as "un-American" or "socialistic" It could be obtained only by creating customer satisfaction (Drucker, 1974).

Another way to help understand purpose in organizational subunits comes out in the Bacone College story. When Charles Holleyman, former president of Bacone, took over, he recalled, "We took every position, including mine, and theoretically fired everyone. Then we started placing them back and justifying their positions (*Tulsa World*).

What they did in effect was to determine the purpose each function had to offer in terms of its overall contribution. If it couldn't be justified, it was combined with others that were only partially justified.

Statement of Purpose of Tulsa Christian Fellowship

Tulsa Christian Fellowship purpose is to be an expression of the body of Christ (the Church), submitted to the Lord Jesus Christ in all things, patterned after the elements of New Testament church order that are reproducible in our context, and dedicated, through the power of the Holy Spirit:

To evangelize the unconverted to a saving faith in Jesus Christ, to apply the healing gospel of Jesus Christ to all kinds of social and personal sins, diseases, and disorders. —*Matt. 28:19 Prov. 11:30 John 10:10.*

To reproduce the life and character of the risen Christ in a growing congregational expression of the Body of Christ, to disciple participants producing in them wholeness and maturity to develop spiritual leaders who can multiply themselves and meet the needs of others. —*Phil. 2:5-11 Matt. 28:19 II Tim 2:2.*

To adore and glorify God in the liberty of the Holy Spirit through public and private worship, and to administer the sacraments or ordinances. —*Rev. 19:10b I Cor. 6:20 Psa. 150 Matt. 28:19 I Cor 11:23-34.*

To experience and express love as the intended relationship of God and man, and man and man. —*John 13:34-35 Matt. 22:37-40*

To encourage and strengthen other expressions of the Body of Christ, especially in Tulsa, and to promote unity and harmony in the Body; abd. —*I Cor. 14:12 Rom. 14:29*

To discover, nurture, and commission people whom the Holy Spirit has called to minister beyond Tulsa. —*Matt. 28:19 Matt. 9:37*

Another example is the proposed purpose statement for Samba's in the early 1980s.

The mission of Samba's Restaurants, a national profit-making company and a leading provider of family style dining, is to utilize capital resources to maximize owner and employee wealth. Demonstrating a sense of responsibility to public interest and earning the respect and loyalty of its customers, Sambo's maintains the highest standards of ethics, quality, and service while protecting both the environment and society. Sambo's Restaurants will become the standard by which family style dining is measured.

The late Dr. L. D. Thomas, senior pastor of Tulsa's First United Methodist Church, used a regular Wednesday evening bible study to get the church congregation involved in bible study, prayer, and development of a formal statement of purpose for the church. That purpose statement set the foundation and continued under the direction of Dr. James Buskirk, the current senior pastor. Buskirk does a good job of translating the dream and the plan into his sermons. It is important for all members of an organization to understand the directions being taken.

A purpose statement must include:

1.   What is the business you are in? Example: Colowyo is in coal mining.

2.   What is the scope of the organization? Example: T. D. Williamson is an international corporation.

3.   What need is satisfied in the marketplace? Example: First Methodist Church satisfies the spiritual growth of its members.

4.   Who are your customers? Example: Colowyo serves utilities, steel mills, etc.

5.   Is it profit or nonprofit? Example: Brush Creek Ranch is nonprofit.

6.   What are your ethics? Example: Phillips Petroleum Company is committed to protect the environment.

Gauging the Environment

It is vital for the organization to gauge the environment within which it operates. This stage is that in which you check the pulse of conditions at the current time frame. You look back for trends. You do studies to forecast the future. Care must be taken not to confuse this stage with the assumption base discussed later. Environmental analysis should be standard practice for all organizations, including universities, churches, and nonprofit units. Southwestern Bell Telephone Company asked me to do a study and present to its managers my thoughts on what the business environment would be like in the mid-1980s. This is the type of futuristic inquiry needed to plan for the future. I had the opportunity to talk to Ean Wilson, a futurist for General Electric. His job is to look ahead and tell G.E. what the world will be like.

My own experience and study have convinced me of the importance of realizing that anything that can happen ultimately will happen.

Just five years ago who would have predicted the dramatic fall of the televangelists? I remember conducting a planning seminar for dentists years ago. At that time tooth decay/treatment was a major revenue generator for dentists. Look how fluoride has transformed their business.

As late as 1970 few would have believed there would be an oil embargo, one energy crisis after another, and the shift in economic power. What this is telling us is that we are in effect managing change. The only way we can manage change is to constantly monitor the environment within which we operate. This gives us clues to changes. Examples for a college of business might be the trends we see in education, the nationwide increase in MBA enrollment, the coming decline in college-age young people, faculty salaries, ethical and social responsibility, and increased growth of adult education, to mention a few. The environmental analysis for Colowyo Coal Company resulted in the following data:

1. While initial projections calling for coal output of 1.2 billion tons by 1985 have been scaled back somewhat, planned production increases remain impressive but seemingly within reach.

2. According to estimates obtained from the Bureau of Mines in mid-1977, U.S. coal production is expected to reach 830 million tons by 1980 and 1.05 billion tons in 1985, up from 671 million tons in 1976.

3. U.S. has coal reserves containing more than 10,000,000 trillion Btu's.

4. Of the 10 largest steam coal companies, which accounted for roughly 45 percent of 1976's domestic steam coal output, three were associated with oil companies (Continental Oil, Occidental Petroleum, and Gulf Oil), three with utilities (American Electric Power, Pacific Power & Light, and Montana Power), one with a mining company (AMAX INC.), and one with a railroad (Burlington Northern).

5. According to a mid-1977 report by the Federal Power Commission (FPC), captive coal's share of utility coal usage is projected to rise to nearly 19 percent in 1985, or about 145 million tons, from about 11 percent in 1976, or around 48.7 million tons. Production at underground mines per man per day fell to 8.50 tons in 1976, from 9.54 tons in 1975.

6. At surface mines, output per man per day dropped to 25.50 tons in 1976, from 26.69 tons in 1975, 33.16 tons in 1974, and 35.71 tons in 1969.

Cross Manufacturing Company, a manufacturer of parts for farm equipment centered in Overland Park, Kansas, provides an example of how environmental analysis is used in the strategic plan. After having used this strategic planning process for approximately a year, major changes started taking place in the marketplace. Higher interest rates and lower commodity prices started having a negative impact on farm income and farm spending.

Some of Cross's major customers, such as International Harvester, started cutting back. Economic conditions got so bad that International Harvester almost went out of business.

It is the job of strategic planning processes to systematically provide management the means to make decisions for tomorrow. How the management system uses the information is another subject. The Cross Manufacturing team recognized that a downturn in business was on them, but assumed that this environmental information was so drastic that a turnaround would be just around the corner. In analyzing the organization's strengths and weaknesses, the management team felt it could hold off a further cut back and be in a position to go into the marketplace much stronger If production and activity were not curtailed. As it worked out, the assumption was erroneous and business activity did not turn around. Some of Cross's major customers like International Harvester found themselves going into an ever deeper hole. The whole chain reaction of high interest rates, depressed farm income, Russian grain embargoes, and other factors caused a slack demand for farm equipment. This caused problems for the International Harvesters and their suppliers such as Cross Manufacturing. The latter used the Strategic Planning System improperly and got caught in making an incorrect assumption.

All companies and organizations must study the present business climate so that they can make good decisions for future activity.

Profit Management Information Systems (PMIS) sells computer based accounting and information systems to oil jobbers. Their success is dependent on a number of factors that include the profitability of its customers, the oil jobbers. There were other environmental factors that during the early eighties would be considered by petroleum-related companies:

1. Crude oil supplies have become plentiful—it is now a buyers' market *(Standard & Poor's,* 7 May 1981:47).

2. Saudis are flooding the market and new production from non-OPEC areas such as Mexico, the North Sea, and Egypt is adding to the glut *(Standard & Poor's,* 7 May 1981:47).

3. Net earnings fell 17 percent, reflecting current industry trends with losses in marketing production caused by high crude oil prices and falling consumption *(Moody's Handbook,* Summer 1981).

4. On January 28, 1981, President Reagan decontrolled the price of crude oil, gasoline, and propane *(Wall Street Journal,* 29 January 1981: 1).

5. An increase in oil production next year was projected by the Independent Petroleum Association of America *(Tulsa Tribune,* 20 October 1981:1b).

6. Increased foreign and domestic taxes, among other things, reduced 1980 profits in the oil industry *(Moody's Handbook,* Summer 1981).

Like Cross Manufacturing, PMIS was faced with planning in a market with unfavorable environmental factors. These factors must be considered along with the present strengths and weaknesses of the company before good, measurable objectives and strategies can be developed.

An example of environment analysis for the food and restaurant industry is the trend of America toward eating more and more meals outside the home. Since 1970, restaurant sales have risen from 42.8 billion dollars to the present 227.3 billion dollars in 1989. In 1985, restaurant sales were 178.4 billion dollars.

That's a 50 billion dollar increase in four years. This is information that needs to be considered if you are looking at that business.

Obviously there are many more factors to consider. Companies like Samba's in 1981 could see the obvious trend. By 1985 overall restaurant sales went from 119.6 billion to 178.4 billion. We know what happened to Samba's during that period; they went out of business. A positive trend doesn't guarantee success at Samba's (*USA Today*, 26 Sept. 1989).

Environmental factors that Samba's considered in 1981:

1. Nation's 100 largest food service companies double market share to 44 percent in 1980 compared to 24 percent in 1970. (*Foods Market*, August 81:8.)

2. Food service industry sales will grow 82 percent from $115 billion in 1979 to $400 billion in 1995. (*Food Stuffs*, 27 April 81:10.)

3. Food service industry will rise from third to first place in domestic retail sales by 1987. (*Foods Products*, January 81:18.)

4. Full service restaurants increasingly use early bird special dinners at low prices to fill tables. (*Nations Restaurants*, 2 March 81:3.)

5. Denny's fast food chain installed distributed processing networks. (*Laser Focus*, August 81:99.)

6. Restaurant chains boosted advertising outlays in 1981 to exceed $456 million in 1979. (*Nations Restaurants*, 25 May 81:1.)

7. Congress passed a bill that allows restaurateurs to offer cash-paying patrons unlimited discounts. (*Nations Restaurants*, 3 August 81:6.)

8. Single person households are shifting toward fast-food restaurants for eating out. (*Nations Restaurants*, 13 April 81:2.)

The purpose of the environmental analysis stage in the Strategic Planning Process gives the organization managers a complete understanding of what they are facing in the marketplace to be successful. The following is from Newman and Logan, *Strategy, Policy, and Central Management,* summary for Chapter 2:

> An essential part of company strategy is a plan for adapting company action to its environment. This is no simple matter because the environment is continuously changing. New technology, social shifts, political realignments and pressures, as well as the more commonly recognized economic changes, all create problems and opportunities. The many examples of exciting new developments noted indicate how dynamic the setting of business is. To adjust most effectively, central management should try to predict important changes before they occur. And these predictions should not only identify the

new factors, they also should anticipate how such shifts in the dynamic environment will affect the company.

Industry surveys, marketing research, Dow Jones stock averages, and recent commodity prices are all environmental factors. When we get up in the morning we look to check the weather. This affects our plans for the day, what we wear, etc. It is in this same vein that a company wants to check external conditions before proceeding with a plan.

In practice, no company can systematically monitor every part of its environment that might change. The task is too big. So the process involves: (1) identifying crucial aspects of the dynamic environment, (2) selecting a forecasting method and making frequent forecasts for each of these aspects, and (3) taking steps to ensure that company executives actually use the forecast in formulating plans.

Since the ability to make good long-range forecasts is limited, especially in the technical-social-political areas, management needs arrangements for frequent measurement. Built-in flexibility in the planning mechanisms is also needed. In other words, the total managing process that this paper examines is no one-time affair. It is a recycling, never ending, and challenging undertaking.

A helpful way to relate shifts in the dynamic environment to current operations of a company is to move first from the general environment to an industry analysis, and then to assess how the particular company stands in that industry.

In this environmental-analysis stage we look at the past, identify trends, and in effect take the pulse of the environment in which the organization operates. Environmental analysis should not be confused with our assumption base discussed later.

Industry studies done by the associations, universities, and the Standard & Poor's Industry Surveys are other examples of information generated for environmental analysis. They represent valuable starting points for the environmental analysis. Another step in a thorough analysis is a complete audit of the organization. There are a number of audits, but the best I have seen is the "General Survey Outline" done by McKinsey in his 1922 book, *Budgetary Control*.

Thomas H. Naylor of Duke University has developed a questionnaire called The Planning Audit that presents a method for auditing the planning system. It reviews the planning environment, organization structure, management philosophy and style, planning process, and other organization factors. The result is a thorough understanding of the strengths and weaknesses of the planning system. It differs from McKenzie's work in that McKenzie's is a complete audit of the organization, whereas Naylor's work is an audit of the planning system (Stevenson, 1976).

Environmental analysis also includes the classification of products in the product life cycle. The product life cycle classifies the firm's existing products on a continuum from R&D through introduction, growth, maturity, and the decline stage. For example, Liberty Industries classified wood pallets in the mature stage of the product life cycle. Recognizing this "cash cow" in mature stage helped them see the long term importance of developing their machinery packaging products.

As we went through this exercise, another client, who asked to remain anonymous, discovered that all of their products were in mature and growth stages. There was an obvious gap coming in three to four years. They immediately made the decision to put more resources into R&D. The vice president of R&D told me privately that after 39 years with the company it was the first time he and his division felt like they were part of the team. The continuing emphasis in this book is team work. All segments of the organization must be in on developing the overall plan.

Here are examples of two environmental factors in 1990. William K. MacReynolds, forecasting director for the U.S. Chamber of Commerce, said the report "shows that the economy has no clear direction," and that "Florida led all states in the nation last year and Orlando ranked fourth among metropolitan areas in landing new corporate facilities and expansions of existing businesses." The rankings were published in *Site Selection Handbook,* a publication produced by Conway Data, Inc., a publisher of economic development news. The survey considered only new corporate facilities and expansions meeting at least one of three criteria: an investment of at least $1 million, creation of at least 50 jobs, or at least 20,000 square feet of new space. This report stated the top 10 states in 1989 in new plants/expansions are Florida, California, Alabama, North Carolina, Texas, Ohio, Pennsylvania, New York, Virginia, and Georgia. The top five metro areas in 1989 in new plants/expansions are Dallas/Fort Worth, Portland, Oregon, Atlanta, Orlando, and Los Angeles/Long Beach (*The Orlando Sentinel*, 1976). Forecasts for the future are included in environmental analysis. Here are some that were made this year in *The Futurist,* the magazine of the World Future Society: By the year 2100, the number of U.S. banks will be fewer than 100, compared with about 15,000 in the 1980s. The number of Americans over age 75 will grow by almost 35 percent by the year 2000. Managers study this data and base their plans on what they think will happen and include assumptions.

Long-Range Planning/MHO Audit

Sections:

I.   Purpose

      A.   Is it written?

      B.   Show purpose as written, or develop one.

      C.   How is the purpose statement being used?

II.   Environmental Analysis

      A.   National trend

      B.   Industry trend

      C.   Go to library and get facts

III.   Strengths and Weaknesses

      A.   Human

      B.   Financial

      C.   Market position

      D.   Facilities

      E.   Equipment

IV.   Assumptions: list at least four

V.   Functional Analysis: list each as strength and/or weakness.

      A.   Financial analysis

          1.   Analyze current financial situation via financial statements.

          2.   What tools would be beneficial in analysis.

              a.   Pro forma statements

              b.   Cash budget

              c.   Capital budget

              d.   Ratio analysis

              e.   Operating and/or financial leverage

              f.   Time value of money

              g.   Break even (C.V.P.)

              h.   Rate of returns

              i.   Project stock and/or bond prices

    3. Analysis of current financial policies

       a. Cash policies

       b. Accounts receivable

         i. Factoring

         ii. Discounts

         iii. Aging schedule

         iv. Collections

       c. Accounts payable

         i. Discounts

       d. Inventory levels

       e. Debt retirement

       f. Dividends/retained earnings

    4. Synopsis of current financial situation.

B. Accounting analysis

    1. Analysis of current accounting policies

       a. Depreciation

       b. Tax considerations

       c. Decentralized/centralized operations

       d. Responsibility accounting

    2. Tools beneficial in analysis

       a. Budgeting (short- and long-range)

       b. Variance analysis

       c. Break even (C.V.P.)

       d. Costing methods

       e. Contribution margin analysis

    3. Synopsis of current accounting situation

C. Market analysis

    1. Analysis of current marketing policies

       a. Consumer

       b. Competition

       c. Product (type of product, type of demand, market position)

       d. Distribution channels

       e. Pricing (markups, discounts, commissions, contributions, etc.)

       f. Promotion (advertising, selling, budget policies)

       g. Profit analysis (variable productions and/or promotion levels)

    2. Synopsis of current market situation

   D. Management analysis

       1. Planning: Do they have a planning system? How does it work?

       2. Organize: Is organization of resources correct? (Show present organizational chart)

       3. Direct: Centralized or decentralized?

       4. Staff: What needs do they have for people?

       5. Control: Are controls in evidence? What are they?

       6. Is there a motivation problem?

       7. Is strategy defined? What is strategy now?

       8. Synopsis of management situation

       9. How efficient is production?

       10. Analyze
            a. Quality control
            b. Production control
            c. Engineering
            d. Maintenance
            e. All major departments
       11. Synopsis of current management situation

As I discussed earlier, McKinsey wrote the "General Survey Outline" in 1936 to accomplish many of the same things (Blake and Mouton, 1972). His outline is more comprehensive and detailed. If an organization has the time and resources to go through the General Survey Outline, it has advantages over this shorter analysis. It is at this stage that the organization is set for making assumptions.

A complete study of the organization industry, products, management, policies, and procedures is needed. Also included in this environmental analysis is a study of the management system outlined in chapter 13. The management questionnaire gives management information on the effectiveness of the management system and brings major problems to the surface. Also discussed is concept of organization culture and how culture affects performance.

Strengths and Weaknesses

After we have identified our purpose and considered the environment in which we operate, we must assess the strengths and weaknesses of our organization. Howard H. Stevenson states, "Business organizations have certain characteristics and strengths which make them uniquely adapted to carry out their tasks. Conversely, they have other features-weaknesses which inhibit their abilities to fulfill their purposes. Managers who hope to accomplish their tasks are forced to evaluate the strengths and weaknesses of the organization (Blake and Mouton, 1972). Some of the things normally looked at would be your key resources: human, financial, facilities/equipment, natural resources/patents, product line, and others. The controller must analyze the financial statements and break out the strengths and weaknesses. It is relatively easy to identify the strengths in each. When you attempt to define weaknesses, it becomes a little more painful. Often organizations must call in outside consultants to be able to candidly pinpoint their limitations. But weaknesses and limitations must be recognized before you move on. You can't develop an achievable plan without knowing your strengths and weaknesses.

One good method to ascertain and bring out strengths and weaknesses is to have the management team break into five discussion groups. Each group is charged with the responsibility of determining strengths and weaknesses in seven areas: Human, Financial, Facilities,/Equipment, Natural Resources/ Patents, Product Lines, and Other.

Strengths and weaknesses can be determined with the use of the worksheets on the following pages. Whatever you wish to measure is classified into one of four categories: dog, problem child, star, or cash cow. For example, a product line with high potential and high performance is a "star." A product line with high potential and low performance is a "problem child."

Blake and Mouton have developed a six-volume series on how to assess the strengths and weaknesses of a business enterprise. It allows the manager to go even deeper into assessing this important area. The series fits logically at this point in the planning process. It helps the manager assess strengths and weaknesses in operations, marketing and sales, research and development, personnel management, financial management, and corporate leadership (Blake and Mouton, 1972).

Before considering the development of a Strategic Planning MBO System, the organization must consider the following factors: (1) Is the organization's management style compatible with the strategic planning MBO process? (2) Is there sufficient backing by the chief executive officer to implement the planning process? (3) Is the organization willing to stay with getting the planning system started long enough to give it a fair trial?

Important Points to Remember

1. The first and most important consideration of a long-range plan is to define the purpose of the organization or any specific part of it.

2. The organization must gauge the environment within which it operates.

3.   Strengths and weaknesses of the organization must be realistically assessed.

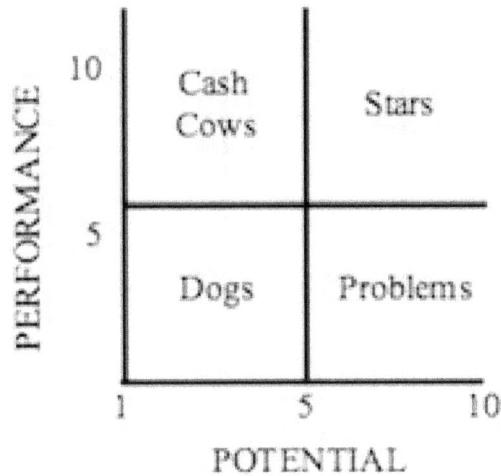

10	Cash Cows	Stars
5	Dogs	Problems
	1 — 5 — 10	

PERFORMANCE (vertical axis) — POTENTIAL (horizontal axis)

This basic evaluation tool can help an organization evaluate a wide range of things. The organization can evaluate production lines, people, facilities, buildings,etc.

Product Lines

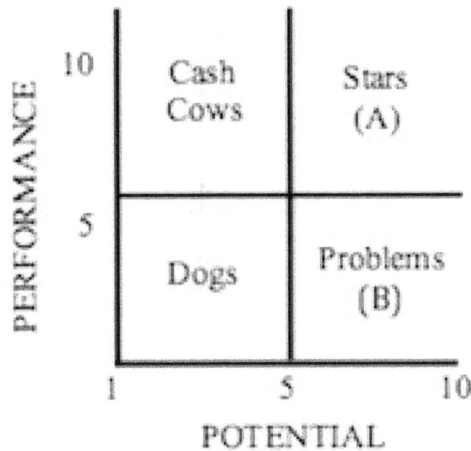

10	Cash Cows	Stars (A)
5	Dogs	Problems (B)
	1 — 5 — 10	

PERFORMANCE (vertical axis) — POTENTIAL (horizontal axis)

For example, Product Line A might be a star with (8.7) rating. B might be a problem with a (8.4) rating.

```
         10 │  Cash        │
            │  Cows        │   Stars
PERFORMANCE │              │
          5 ├──────────────┼──────────────
            │  Dogs        │
            │  (C)         │   Problems
            │              │
            └──────────────┴──────────────
            1              5              10
                  POTENTIAL
```

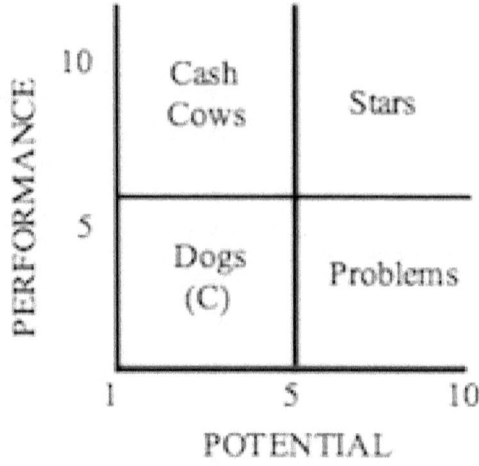

For example, Production Line C would be a dog if it had a (3.3) rating. Human Resources

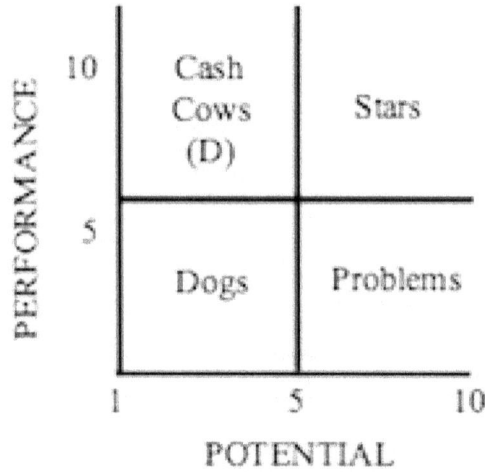

```
         10 │  Cash        │
            │  Cows        │   Stars
            │  (D)         │
PERFORMANCE ├──────────────┼──────────────
          5 │              │
            │  Dogs        │   Problems
            │              │
            └──────────────┴──────────────
            1              5              10
                  POTENTIAL
```

3.   Strengths and weaknesses of the organization must be realistically assessed.

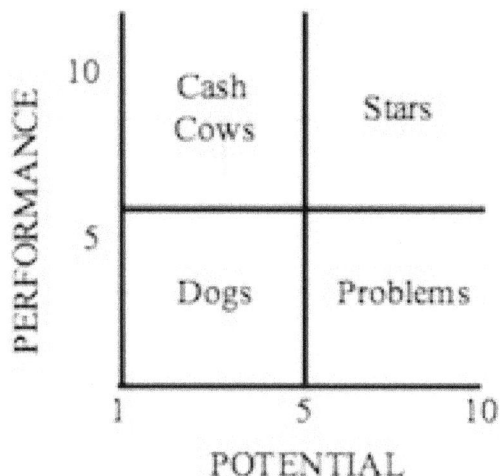

This basic evaluation tool can help an organization evaluate a wide range of things. The organization can evaluate production lines, people, facilities, buildings,etc.

Product Lines

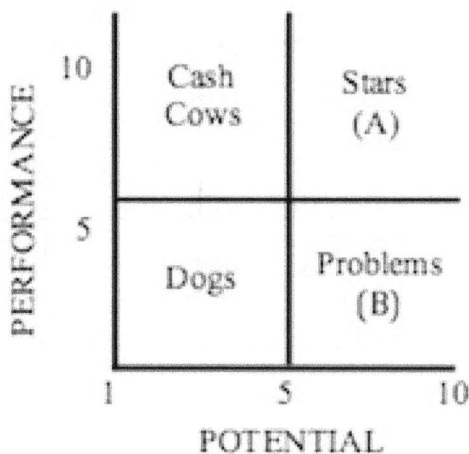

For example, Product Line A might be a star with (8.7) rating. B might be a problem with a (8.4) rating.

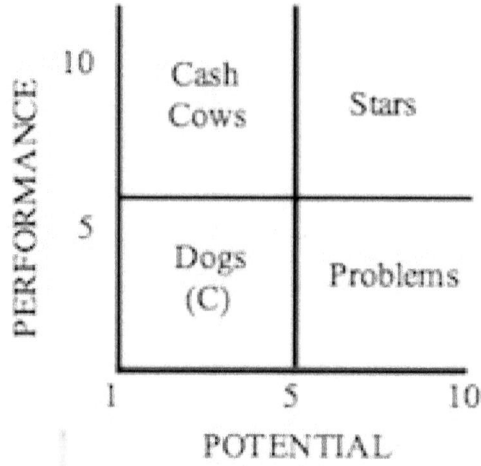

For example, Production Line C would be a dog if it had a (3.3) rating.
Human Resources

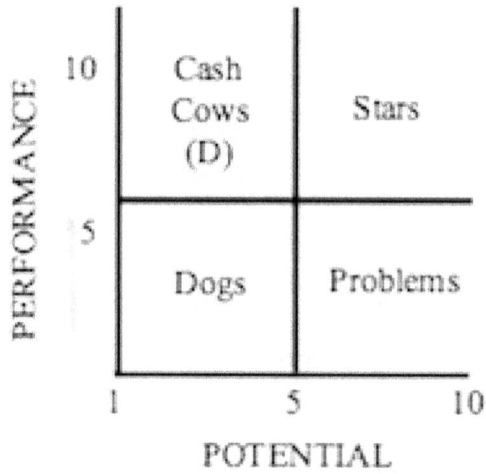

For example, Person D might be a (3.8) a cash cow.

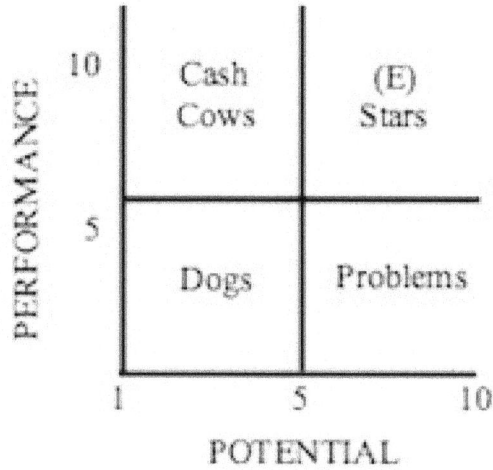

For example, a new plant, well laid out, might be E, a (9.9) a star.

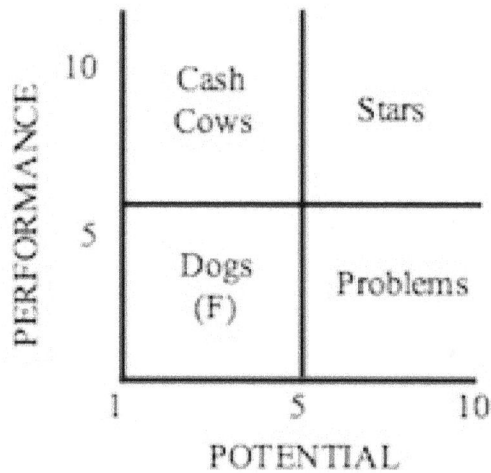

For example, a piece of machine (F) might have a (3.3) rating and be classified as a "dog."

References

Blake, Robert R.. and Jane S. Mouton. *How to Assess the Strengths and Weaknesses of a Business Enterprise*. Austin: Scientific Methods, Inc. 1972. A six-volume series.

Business Success Story, *Tulsa World*.

Drucker, Peter. *Management*. New York: Harper & Row. 1984: 79.

Ibid., 75

Humble, John. "Social Responsibility—The Contribution of MBO." *MBO Journal*. Vol. 5, No. 3:1969.

McKinsey, J.O. *Budgetary Control*. New York: The Ronald Press Company. 1922:52-94.

Standard & Poor's Industry Surveys, Standard & Poor's Corp., 345 Hudson Street, New York: 10014.

Stevenson, Howard H. "Defining Corporate Strengths and Weaknesses," *Sloan Management Review*, Spring 1976: 52-67.

The Orlando Sentinel, "Economic Barometer Levels Off," 3 March, 1990. See B, p. 1.

CHAPTER 3
ASSUMPTIONS, OBJECTIVES, PERFORMANCE CONTRACTS, AND WAYS TO MEASURE SUCCESS

You cannot achieve goals if you don't have any;
if not you look at the past and wonder where it went.

Evelyn Roberts

This chapter deals with making assumptions, writing objectives, negotiating objectives, and agreeing on objectives to form a performance contract. You should be able to explain the reasoning behind making assumptions before writing your objectives. Furthermore, you should be able to write objectives and be able to discuss the concept of the performance contract. This chapter covers these topics in detail.

Assumptions

You should make your major assumptions about spheres over which you have little or absolutely no control—for example, the external environment. A good way to start is to extend some of the items studied in the environmental analysis.

Should the assumption stage appear to be relatively unimportant in developing a long-range plan, consider the following:

1. If by studying the environment of a college of business it would be assumed there would be a drop-off in demand for the MBA, the school would not have had an objective of hiring one more faculty member.

2. More than likely all the automotive companies have assumed that no oil embargo will be imposed next year. Consider how their plans and objectives would change if they assumed an embargo was in the offing.

3. A few years ago I was leading a planning session for a major oil company. At that time they assumed $35/barrel for oil.

Some PMIS assumptions from their 1984 plan:

1. The oil glut will continue until mid-1984.

2. Interest rates will stay above 15 percent for another year.

3. Profit margins for oil jobbers will stay tight.

4.   The predictions of some economists is correct and the turnaround in activity will not come until 1984.

Assumptions for most organizations for 1990 could likely be:

1.   There will be a continued lowering of the prime rate to about 10 percent.

2.   There will be no major labor strikes.

3.   West Texas Inter-market crude will be in the $18-$20 range.

These assumptions could be included in the strategic plan for GISI. Because PMIS is a supplier of computer and accounting systems to oil jobbers, their assumptions extended from the environmental analysis greatly affect the objectives and strategies to be set later in their strategic plan. All of these assumptions seem to indicate tight markets and margins for the customers of PMIS. These environmental factors and assumptions then become the basis for developing sound, measurable, and obtainable objectives. Because of this situation, PMIS is developing strategies to provide more services to current customers rather than to emphasize the gaining of new customers. In order for GISI to meet its long-term sales and production objectives, this strategy of concentration on its current customers makes sense because of the environmental conditions and the assumption that these conditions are going to stay the same.

This is a key example of how the management team must use different steps in the strategic planning process as a base on which to make decisions in other steps of the process. If, for example, the environmental analysis showed a period of prosperity, high gross national product, tight oil supplies, and high profit margins such as those evidenced in the embargo era of the mid-1970s, then an assumption could be made that these conditions would remain the same over the next operating period. If that were the case, then the GISI management would probably develop a strategy to go after more new customers with positive cash positions.

It should also be noted that the top management team must indicate the assumptions in the strategic plan that have the most opportunity and risk for the organization. If any of those key assumptions are incorrect, then a contingency plan must be developed to handle the unexpected assumption change.

An example of a contingency plan is that made by a group of students on a class project for the City of Tulsa. The city government assumed after the oil embargo that there would not be another embargo. However, at the time the threat of another embargo seemed to me to be great enough to require a contingency plan that could be implemented immediately if tight petroleum supplies should again prevail. A detailed contingency plan was developed and agreed on. Every department knew specifically how to react if supplies were cut drastically. For example, the routes and frequency rates for the city trash pickup, police traffic patterns, and other areas of fuel consumption were provided with a plan that could be immediately implemented If needed. William L. Schubert, an economist from California, has done extensive study on business cycles. An organization uses specialists like Schubert in the environmental analysis state. The organization then makes its own assumptions, perhaps agreeing and building elements of its plan around these assumptions.

Rate of change trend analysis suggests that 1990 will be a good but unexciting year for the economy. Interest rates will cycle mildly within their present range, the stock market will continue to rise despite intermittent declines, and business activity will begin to re-accelerate in the first quarter. Consumer price inflation will oscillate between 4.5 and 5 percent with no sign of blow-off. Very long term analysis shows that inflation is now on the down side of the long 54-year cycle. There is no reason why the current growth rates cannot be maintained provided the government doesn't do anything foolish. The entire decade can be one of continuous, vigorous growth as we now come out of the low point of the long Kondratieff economic wave.

Some years ago the Public Service Company of Oklahoma wanted to develop a procedure for monitoring and identifying significant internal data series which might signal need for management attention. The task force assigned to the project decided that ROC Trend Analysis would be the best means of identifying and focusing attention on critical areas. Starting with the monthly operating statement, all important categories of revenue, product sales, expenses, and other various operating ratios were converted to rates of change with an analytic report prepared once every quarter. More than 80 series were monitored, compared, and analyzed. The first report was compiled in 1983, and rate of change charts showed graphically that expenses were growing at a much more rapid rate than revenues and that the rate of growth was accelerating. While the data came from accounting statements, the import was not obvious, but the problem was made immediately apparent by the extreme divergence in growth rates made dramatically evident by the ROC curves. Martin Fate, president of PSO, observed that the rate of change analyses gave him insights he had not had before. Fate emphasized the value of the methodology, saying, "We instituted significant cost control measures and a new resource allocation process which enables us to continually improve our planning, primarily as a result of ROC Trend Analysis. The result has been a one-time reduction of total expenses by 11 percent with even greater improvement of profits."

The assumption may seem elementary, but it must be done. It helps you to identify all the important factors that you feel will remain constant. If any one of them changes drastically, major revisions in plans might be needed. As an exercise, list the assumptions for your organization on a separate piece of paper.

Objectives and Goals

Management by objectives (MBO) has caused a stir in all areas of organizational life over the past 40 years. It is well to remember that the word management is the key. Management by objectives is the use of objectives to help manage for results. Before any discussion of writing objectives can begin, we must again refer to the new definition of MBO presented in chapter 1. The purpose of the organization must be defined, environmental analysis made, strengths and weaknesses assessed, and assumptions made. Then and only then can objectives be considered. The examples that follow are from a wide range of industries.

Objectives must be clear, concise, written statements outlining what is to be accomplished in a key priority area, in a certain time period, in measurable terms that are consistent with the overall objectives of the organization.[1] Objectives can be classified as routine, problem-solving, innovative, team, personal, and budgetary. Drucker feels that "objectives are not fate; they are direction. They are not commands; they are commitments (Drucker, 1974). They do not determine the future; they are means to mobilize the resources and energies of the business for the making of the future. Without objectives we tend to fall into managing by habit, staying busy in an "activity trap," as Odiorne often refers to it. We have a tendency to work hard, not smart. Objectives help you to see where you are going. Evelyn Roberts (1977) has said:

> You can't achieve goals if you don't have any. Sometimes this idea is so simple that many people pass it by. In order to accomplish anything, we've got to first propose in our hearts to do it. We've got to make up our minds. If we don't, we just waste our time and energy and find ourselves going around in circles, looking back at the past and wondering where it went.

Objectives are those clear, measurable targets. You don't just get in your car and drive somewhere. Family members agree to go somewhere, perhaps to dinner and have a destination in mind at a certain time. Plans can be organized when you know where you are going, dress and distance are all considered. How many organizations in America are "just going for a drive?" No one knows where he is going but works very hard and sometimes is efficient at going nowhere. We need specific measurable objectives to make organizations work. After objectives are set, you develop a strategy to get there, and then you work hard at getting there.

Objectives can be set at upper organizational levels in profitability and growth, market position and penetration, productivity, product leadership, employee morale, development, and attitudes, physical and financial resources, and public responsibility (Mali, 1972). You should set an objective in each of these areas in the long-range plan of your organization or company.

The top management team must set organization objectives in the following areas:

1. Profitability and sales

    a. profit to sales
    b. sales in volume and dollars

2. Production and productivity

    a. units
    b. cost per unit
    c. efficiency

3. Product characteristic

    a. quality
    b. research and development
    c. engineering

4. People

    a. safety
    b. training
    c. management system balance sheet/culture index

5. Financial resources and performance

    a. return on assets
    b. earnings per share
    c. The five to 10 key financial ratios depending on the organization must be set here. An example is the current ratio or inventory turnover.

6. Public responsibility

7. Overall budget

The discussion here centers on objectives in a range of settings. Objectives in these seven areas can be further broken down into routine problem-solving, innovative, personal, team, and budgetary objectives. The study of objectives in these categories is purely academic. I usually emphasize that the organization or unit identify its five to ten most important results. It is a good idea, however, to understand each of the objective types.

Routine Objectives

Routine objectives have to do with those activities, jobs, or work assignments that occur regularly and predictably. An example of a routine objective for the foreman of a machine shop might be: "Complete a preventive maintenance check on all equipment each calendar quarter in 1990." Notice that the objective states what is to be accomplished: "complete a preventive maintenance check" on all equipment in a certain, measurable time period, "each calendar quarter."

Other routine objectives might be:

1. I will spend an average of 15 minutes per week in 1990 discussing safety with my group.

2. I will review each machinist's objectives and accomplishments quarterly.

3. I will attend every department meeting.

Problem-Solving Objectives

Problem-solving objectives identify existing, recognized problem areas and state a time period for solution.

An example of a problem-solving objective for a dental dean might be: "Develop a syllabus and a teaching plan for dental hygiene by August 1990." Other problem-solving objectives might be:

1. Develop a plan for faculty internship with local dentists by January 1990.

2. Develop a set of criteria for admitting dental students by October 1990.

3. Hold a one-day symposium on the spiritual and mental health of dentists and prepare summary minutes and recommendations by November 1990.

Innovative Objectives

Innovative objectives look to the future, suggest a completion date, and usually improve an existing situation. For example, an innovative objective for a personnel manager might be: "Devise a better system of screening new hires by July 1, 1990." Another innovative objective might be: "Develop a method or methods to give supervisors feedback on their performance. At least one method will be implemented by May 1, with another method implemented by June 1."

Personal Objectives

Personal objectives relate directly to the person, and they are those he or she wishes to achieve during the year. Examples for a shipping foreman are:

1. To improve my understanding of management, I will read Dr. Migliore's *MBO: Blue Collar to Top Executive* and attend at least one Executive Action Seminar at Northeastern State University during the fall semester.

2. I will develop a career development plan by October 1990.

Team Objectives

Team objectives are those that need to be accomplished with another member of the organization team. An example for a librarian might be: "I will work with the library consultant to revise our new library classification procedure for law books. We will discuss it in May and introduce the new procedure in July 1990."

Another example might be: "I will work with the library consultant to develop a faster way to handle outside inquiries. We will develop a system by October 1, 1990."

Budgetary Objectives

Budgetary objectives are quantitative, measurable, and usually set on a yearly time frame consistent with the organization's financial year. An example might be: "The Press Department will operate within its $100,000 yearly budget during 1990-91." Budgetary objectives are usually felt to be the most important because of their financial nature, but all other objectives are just as important to support the total MBO program.

How to Measure Performance

One practical, easy way to record, communicate, measure, and update objectives is through a "Performance Plan Book" or "Management Plan Book." All steps in the planning process, including objectives for the organization, are in this book. The objectives are reviewed periodically, usually each quarter, and updated. Table 1 shows how objectives can be listed, kept track of, and presented for review. Each manager reviews his progress on goal attainment each quarter. A Sample college of business objectives and samples from a number of areas are included. This is a method I developed at Continental Can Company in 1967. It greatly reduces paper work and provides a convenient method for review. The planning book is kept up to date by that person in the organization who coordinates the long-range plan.

Now that you have made the assumptions, take time to write objectives in these seven areas. Use the seven areas as guides.

Profitability and Sales			
	Sales	**Percentage Profit/Sales**	**R.O.I.**
1st year			
2nd year			
3rd year			
4th year			
5th year			
Production and Productivity			
	Units	**Cost/Unit**	**Efficiency**
1st year			
2nd year			
3rd year			
4th year			
5th year			
Product Characteristics			
Quality			
R&D			
Engineering			
People			
Safety			
Training			
Management System Balance Sheet			
Financial Resources			
Public Responsibilities			
Overall Budget			

Note the general worksheets on the following pages that suggest areas for objectives. The key is to use these suggested worksheets to find those few that best represent what needs to be measured.

WORKSHEET

	Last Year	Next Year	Five Years
SALES Total sales/revenue Net sales per dollar of net worth Net sales per dollar of total assets Net sales per dollar of net working capital Cost of sales per dollar of inventory Net sales per dollar of depreciated fixed assets			

MARKET POTENTIAL
Percent Market Share
      Regional
      National
      World
Percent Products
      In introductory stage
      In maturity stage
      In declining stage			

MANUFACTURYING/PRODUCTIVITY
Total Output =
      Labor+materials+energy+capital+mi3scella-
neous input
Number projects
      Completed
      Scheduled
Units produced
Hours worked
Sales
Employees
Quality
Customer service			

Labor Productivity
Items produced per employee
Quantities produced per employee-hour
Labor index =

$$\frac{\text{equivalent employee-hours of output}}{\text{actual total employee-hours}} \times 100$$

Labor productivity index =

$$\frac{\text{price weighted output (period 2)} \Big/ \text{total labor costs (period 2)}}{\text{price weighted output (period 1)} \Big/ \text{total labor costs (price 1)}} \times 100$$

Materials Productivity
Output per constant dollar of total material cost

Energy Productivity
Output per energy consumer (BTU's)
Energy productivity index =

$$\frac{\text{output} \Big/ \text{BTU (constant period)}}{\text{output} \Big/ \text{BTU (base period)}} \times 100$$

or
Energy Productivity Index =

$$\frac{\text{output in current period} \Big/ \text{output in base period}}{\text{BTU in current period} \Big/ \text{BTU in base period}} \times 100$$

Capital Productivity Quantity of output per quantity of capital input Capital productivity = $$\frac{\text{quantity of output}}{\text{quantity of capital}} = \frac{\text{units prod./day}}{\text{units inventory}} = \frac{\text{units prod./day}}{\text{machine}}$$ $$\text{of input} \qquad\qquad \text{(process unit)}$$			
People Man-hours worked without lost time from accidents. Various other safety objectives.			
Quality Zero defects Acceptance rates vs. various sampling plans			
FINANCIAL SALES **Return on Investment** Net profit after taxes/net worth Net profit after taxes/total assets Net profit after taxes + depreciation + noncash expense/ total assets			

Return on Sales
Net sales per dollar
      of net worth
      of total assets
      of net working capital
Net profit after taxes/net sales
Cost of sales per dollar of inventory
New sales per dollar of depreciated fixed assets			

Financial Leverage Debt/equity ratio Total debt/total assets Times interest earned			
Current Ratio Current assets to current liabilities Cash and receivables to current liabilities Cash and equivalent to current liabilities Current liabilities to net worth Acid-test ratio (current assets-inventory)/(current liabilities)			

Activity Inventory turnover Accounts receivable turnover Average collection period Total asset turnover Fixed asset turnover			
Market Ratios Earnings per share Dividends per share Dividend payout ratio Book value per share Price/earnings ratio Dividend yield			
FACILITIES Yearly safety check Annual energy audit			
PEOPLE/TRAINING/MORALE Management system balance sheet Yearly people development audit 25 hours training per employee/year Quality circles (participation teams) implemented Turnover Performance/reward system Benefits Compensation levels Wellness Manpower forecast Recruiting objectives and costs Succession planning			
PUBLIC RESPONSIBILITY 100% United Way Sponsor Junior Achievement Co. 200 working days per year volunteers Pay all taxes, wages, and bills Contribute $300,000 to civic projects Meet OSHA safety requirements			

After the president or chief operating officer has gathered the staff to think through the major objectives, the subunit managers must develop their plans and objectives to support the overall objectives. The key subunit persons should be involved in the supporting subunit objectives.

After the top management team has worked through the organizational objectives based on all the previous steps and discussion in the strategic planning process, each subunit manager is beginning to perceive what his organizational unit must do to support the overall plan. After the various strategies are developed for each of the major objectives, the subunit manager must gather his team and go through the same process. At this point, one of two steps can be taken. Each organizational subunit, such as the vice president heading marketing, the vice president of production, and perhaps the controller, can start with step one, the purpose, and develop the purpose, say, for the controller's area. They will work on salient environmental factors in the controller's area, study its unit strengths and weaknesses, make assumptions specifically important to the controller's area, and then develop specific objectives that contribute to the overall strategic plan for the organization. Other organizations I have worked with prefer to let the analysis that has taken place in the organization plan be the stage setting and to go directly into setting objectives for their particular units. For example, A. B. Steen, president of T.D. Williamson, Inc., brings his managers from around the world to Tulsa for a yearly planning meeting. They chart the direction of the company over the long term. Each individual functional manager then develops a game plan to support the overall plan. For example, to achieve the sales volume objective for T.D. Williamson, Inc., the unit managers of the marketing and service divisions set objectives as follows:

- Marketing to increase penetration of the gas distribution market in 1990, to achieve the following share of market by 1994: product A 45%, product B 30%, product C 45%.
- Manufacturing to develop an integrated manufacturing control system by July 1, 1991.
- T.D.W. Services Division to complete the development of a quality control program for all services performed by October 1991.

The concept of an effective objective is not measurable, but it is important. An example from ORU is appropriate. To the degree that the university achieves these purposes and the student responds to these opportunities the student will:

1. Develop a concept of personal honor based on the principles of integrity, common sense, reverence for God, esteem for man, and respect for social and spiritual laws.

2. Develop a sense of responsibility and citizenship, which enhances his or her moral and spiritual growth.

3. Apply himself or herself to the development of the full powers of the mind.

4. Practice good health habits and regularly participate in wholesome physical activities.

5. Employ his or her professional expertise in the world.

6. Endeavor to seek the will of God for his or her life and to exemplify a Christ-like character.

Notice the effective objectives for ORU attained will tend to support the ORU purpose.

Important Points To Remember

1. Without proper objectives, managing is a day-to-day crisis.

2. Direction is difficult if you don't know where you are going.

3. With proper objectives there is a sense of direction.

4. George Morrisey calls objectives the results you wish to achieve.

5. How can you guide and measure a person's performance if you first don't agree on what is to be accomplished?

6. The objectives must be clear, concise, written statements outlining what is to be accomplished in a key priority area, within a time frame, and in measurable terms.

Conclusion

The objectives become a performance contract after they have been:

1. Properly written and submitted to the supervisor

2. Discussed and negotiated with the supervisor

3. Resubmitted to the supervisor

4. Approved by both parties

5. Signed by both parties

The objectives once negotiated are the just measurable results confirmed in the strategic long-range plan. Every precious step was to set the stage for proper long- and short-range measurable targets and results expected.

In my 1986 news column in the *Tulsa Tribune*, I specifically forecast three events by the year 2000. One was an event beyond anyone's imagination in Europe. No, I didn't know the Berlin Wall would come down. My forecast was not that spectacular. More specific, the column called for U.S. involvement in major military action in the mid-east. The Gulf War came along as predicted. The Third was a major worldwide economic downturn year 2000.

Each of these predictions came from a report I developed for a major U.S. corporation. I was asked to report to top management and the board on world conditions and economic situations in the year 2000.

After looking at all the forecasts from 1950-1985, the pattern was obvious. Almost all the economic models crunch their numbers and predict changes in a fairly narrow range. No legitimate service, to my knowledge, predicted the economic highs and lows from 1950 to 1985. Right now you will notice, no one is predicting a high or low. Common sense says there are highs or lows in the future.

Now look at the Kondratieff curve. Very interesting!!! Guess where we are on the cycle? Don't guess, here are the facts. We are on the downward slope of the curve. The 50-55 year cycle of the Kondratieff curve has been on accurate predictions of business cycles.

So what do we do??? Ignore the obvious warnings??!! Full speed ahead? Or is it time for a wake-up call!

The question is how are we going to manage our organizations and personal lives. Who will be in the driver's seat in the year 2010? Should we trust our luck or try to weave your way through the icebergs.

Notes

1. For an excellent view of how company and organizational objectives are set, refer to Dr. Richard Johnson's dissertation, *A Systematic Approach to Long-Range Planning* (1969), North Texas State University. Before objectives can be set, the organization must monitor its environment, make assumptions, set criteria, and assess its strengths and weaknesses. Only then is it in a position to set objectives and goals. Also refer to my book, *MBO: Blue Collar to Top Executive* (Washington: Bureau of National Affairs, 1977) pages 2-3. I suggest defining purpose and then the other stages before objectives are set. Also refer to George Morrisey's book, *Management by Objectives and Results*, pages 62-63, for guidelines and sample objectives. Roger Fritz has excellent educational examples in a manuscript he developed for a conference at ORU entitled, "Colleges Can Be Managed."
2. The Penton Publishing Company Education Division has an excellent MBO cassette/text programmed learning course. It recommends and gives examples for these types of objectives: routing, problem-solving, and innovative.

References

Drucker, Peter. *Management*. New York: Harper & Row. 1974: 102.

Mali, Paul. *Managing Objectives*, New York: Wilby, 1972: 117.

Roberts, Evelyn. *Daily Blessing*. Tulsa: ORU Press. Jan.-Mar. 1977: 10-11.

CHAPTER 4
STRATEGY AND LONG- AND SHORT-RANGE PLANNING

In this chapter, ideas of strategy and long- and short-range planning are discussed. By the end of this chapter you should be able to distinguish between objectives and strategies and should be able to write strategies in order to meet the objectives stated in chapter 4. Also, you should be able to write a long-range plan (five-years) to accomplish the objectives stated, using the strategies set forth.

Finally, you should be able to distinguish between long-range and short-range plans and be able to develop the short-range plan of your five-year plan.

Strategy

After objectives and goals have been set, a strategy must be developed to achieve the goals and objectives. A good way to outline a strategy is to ask yourself: "How and where am I going to commit my resources?" Your answer will be your strategy. Or you might describe strategy as your "game plan. A basketball coach could us a strategy of shifting from a man-to-man defense to a zone press. A university could consider the strategy of allowing "accountable time" to one professor each semester to do proper research. Some examples of marketing strategy are:

1. De-marketing
2. Changes in product mix
3. Changes in price policy
4. Changes in promotional strategy

It is during the strategy phase that we consider organizational structure. Drucker says, "The best structure will not guarantee results and performances. But the wrong structure is a guarantee of nonperformance" (Drucker, 1974).

Strategy also concerns timing. The timing of the introduction of a new product can be very important. An example of strategy in a real estate setting would be the decision whether or not to expand into a new area of a city. Another strategy would be determination of the amount and type of advertising. Remember that strategy is not "doing." It is the thinking process. The "doing" comes in the five-year and one-year operation plans. For more information on strategy, refer to Hanna (1975), Richards and Nielander (1969), and Hutchinson (1971).

The strategy phase begins to receive more and more attention after the organization has been on the strategic planning process the second and third year. Until this time, most of the attention has gone into the previous steps. This is not to say that strategic decisions haven't been made, and in many cases, made properly. We all use strategy daily. We are looking into the environment when we arise in the morning, look outside, and make an assumption on how the weather might change as we make the strategic decision of what to wear that day and whether or not to take an umbrella. Organizations used strategy long before they recognized the need for overall planning. What the strategic planning/MBO process is doing is creating the framework so that when strategy decisions are made, they are made within the context of the overall business situation. As we have seen, specific strategies must be developed for the overall key corporate objectives. Another example of strategy is Sears Roebuck & Company's going into the field of financial services. Sears obviously has had objectives to attain sales in the 18 billion range. Using a planning system, Sears appears to have recognized the environmental factors already discussed here. They had to recognize that their profits have tumbled since 1977, and were faced with a tougher job in meeting the overall sales and profits objectives needed for the company to survive. Within this framework, it appears that they have decided to commit resources and that they believe the timing was correct to introduce financial services into their product mix. They are taking advantage of one of their great strengths, which is the confidence of the American consumer and the millions of people who regularly patronize the Sears stores. I believe this has been a well-considered strategic move. Using its customer base for carefully targeted loans and other financial services should bolster the company's profitability (*Business Week*, 1981).

Colowyo general strategies include buildup of production capacity, and buying equipment needed for future operations at attractive prices caused by the downturn in the copper and uranium industries. Bendix Corporation at one time kept about one-sixth of its assets in the bank and in liquid securities. Bendix earned attractive interest while looking for the right opportunities to use the cash to help the company.

Another example of strategy is the difficult question of pricing. In spite of all the sophisticated pricing models, it appears that the pricing decision cannot be scientifically determined. In some cases, the higher the price of certain products, such as a luxury car or some other status product, the more desirable the product becomes. When J.C. Penney Company went into its "plain pockets" jeans and its shirts with the fox emblems, it was an example of price-cutting strategy against the Levi Strauss & Company's jeans and alligator shirts. The strategy was that the lower price would result in a more profitable product line (*Wall Street Journal*, 1981).

An example of strategy in the food business is Wendy's strategy on their hamburger. In order to combat McDonalds' frozen, pre-cooked, and warmed hamburger, Wendy's wanted to have a hamburger cooked on the spot. There is risk in continually cooking hamburgers. If they are not consumed fresh and on the spot, they become tomorrow's Wendy's chili.

Another example of strategy in the food/restaurant business has been the drive-through window. Coupons, sales, and price reductions such as Arby's five hamburgers for $5 after 5:00 p.m. are strategies. Some characteristics of a successful strategy are: (1) it is understood by all in the organization; (2) it is flexible; and (3) it reacts to changes in the environment and assumptions.

In the strategic phase, the organization must recognize its driving force. Benjamin B. Tregoe, chairman and CEO of Kepner-Tregoe, Inc., says this:

> The notion of driving force is crucial to the strategy formulation and implementation process.
>
> Briefly, driving force is the primary determiner of the scope of future products and markets of an organization. Determining driving force will help the top team answer such questions as "Why are we in our current businesses and not others? Why are we making the products we are making and not others?"
>
> Research suggests that there are nine possible driving forces. Here are the nine:(1) products offered, (2) market needs, (3) technology, (4) production capability, (5) method of sale, (6) method of distribution, (7) natural resources, (8) size-growth, and (9) return profit.

A major area is in the planning gap. The planning gap is represented in the diagram below.

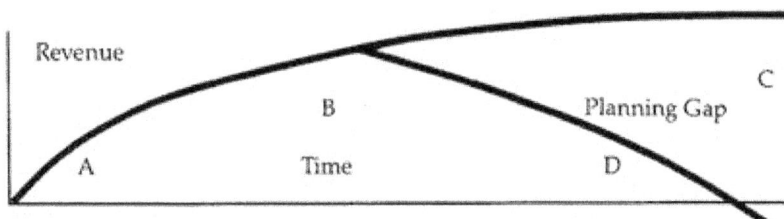

With the firm's total revenue on the vertical axis and time being represented by the horizontal axis, we can see the planning gap concept. The total revenue curve, ABD, is what a company can expect in returns from its present products and services. At the present rate of innovations, inventories, and improvements, all these things begin to become obsolete. Notice the BD portion of the curve.

What the firm must have is continuing revenues represented by the curve of ABC, expressed in terms of an objective. The gap between BC and BD can be overcome only by good planning, which is done at the strategy stage of long-range planning/MBO. After the objectives are set on sales or total revenue following the ABC objective, management must then develop the specific strategy or game plan to achieve this result.

T. D. Williamson Inc. has a good planning system started by the late Ed Green in the mid-1970s. Green was a recognized leader in the planning field. The company was founded by the late T. D. Williamson, Sr., passed on to his son, T. D. Williamson, Jr., and now is headed by the very capable A. B. Steen. Steen is the type of chief executive officer who can get the most out of the planning process. He practices what he preaches, sets objectives, measures people by their results, and rewards accordingly.

He asked me to lead his company's 1979 planning conference. The main theme after setting the stage was to develop specific strategies to overcome the planning gap. Good solid objectives were set through 1985. Steen then turned the conference over to me to bring out the opinions and creativity of the management team. Not many chief executive officers have the courage and confidence to show this type of participation. We arrived at four specific strategies. I am sure you can perceive the commitment the T. D. Williamson management team will have in implementing their strategies. How would the management team feel If outside consultants came in and worked with Steen to develop the strategy for the company? They would not have liked it!

One strategy developed at T. D. Williamson was to move company operations to where the customers are located. The strategy to move company operations to the Mideast and Southeast Asia was developed.

As an exercise, the reader can develop a set of strategies to meet each of the objectives.

Operational Plans: Long- and Short-Range

After all the steps have been taken and a strategy has been developed to meet our objectives and goals, it is time to develop both long- and short range plans. Examples of long-range plans are found in building, equipping, hiring people, developing curriculum, and so on. It is important not to confuse the long- and short-range plan with strategy. This is the *action* or *doing* stage. Strategy was the thinking stage. Here you hire, fire, build, advertise, and so on. In every long-range plan I have ever been involved with, we have developed pro forma income and balance sheets for five years. We also have developed contribution analysis by product line for five years. The sales forecast for five years should also be included in this section. In manufacturing, the master production control schedule fits this area. For maintenance, the overhaul and preventive maintenance schedule fits here also.

Personnel managers can line up training activities and plans for all their people over the next five years in this section. Ideally, each person has assessed his strengths and weaknesses and then set his own training and self-improvement objectives.

In short, a five-year operating plan must be developed for every function of the business. Marketing, finance, personnel, accounting, manufacturing, etc. must develop a plan that insures the success of the overall company plan. When the objectives in chapter 4 are set for the organization and strategies are developed, each organizational unit must do its part to insure that it makes the proper contribution to the success of the plan.

Zero-Base Budgeting in a Short-Range Plan

There has been a big movement toward zero-base budgeting (ZBB) in recent years. Allen Austin found in a survey of 481 enterprises that there are definite benefits to zero-base budgeting. Zero-base budgeting has a natural fit in the planning process. It probably is more applicable in business than in government, where the results have been mixed. Zero-base budgeting can be defined as follows:

> The basic concept of attempting to reevaluate all programs and expenditures every year, hence the term zero-base, is not new. The process requires each manager to justify his entire budget request in detail and puts the burden of proof on him to justify why he should spend any money (Pyhrr, 1973).

Former President Carter defined zero-base budgeting this way:

> In contrast to the traditional budgeting approach of incrementing the new on the old, zero-base budgeting demands a total rejustification of everything from zero. It means chopping up the organization into individual functions and analyzing each annually, regardless of whether it is 50 years old or a brand-new proposal for a future program (Carter, 1977).

The budget is broken into units called decision packages, prepared by managers at each level. These packages cover every existing or proposed activity of each department. They include analyses of purpose, costs, measures of performance and benefits, alternative courses of action, and consequences of disapproval.

Zero-base budgeting can be summarized as a further sophistication of the regular budgeting process. Every expenditure and activity is rejustified at the budget proposal stage. Those activities and functions that have been part of the organization's regular activities are thought through again.

As Peter Drucker in 1954 was given credit for putting all the elements of management by objectives together, it appears that Peter A. Pyhrr has been the one key person to put all the elements of zero-base budgeting together in his book, *Zero-Base Budgeting*, published in 1973 (Pyhrr, 1973).

It is in this stage that ZBB and MBO most logically fit together. The yearly budget and activities that go along with the budget under MBO are the first year of the five-year plan. I see that ZBB, with its yearly "let's start from point zero" requirement would make units and subunits reanalyze their purpose or reason for being.

Because the yearly budget is entrenched in our organized society (families, government, industry, and nonprofit groups), ZBB could be the catalyst to force more and better long-range planning. Every manager in every organization is sensitive to his budget, and ZBB then becomes the mechanism to force him to learn to manage with his budget. Too many units see the budget as only "What do we have to spend?" and then find ways to spend it. We need to move to "What needs to be done?" and then "How much does it cost?"

It seems more logical to me for the organizational unit to define its purpose, analyze its environment, its strengths, its weaknesses, and to make a few key assumptions. Then it sets its objectives and makes up a strategy and plan to meet these objectives. Top management then submits a five-year budget that represents the cost to implement that plan. Then and only then can the first year's budget be judged on its merit. Top management needs to see what the subunit can produce and what its cost will be. Accountability needs to be forced into the budget process. Once the budget is agreed on, the unit manager freely manages his part of it. If he can't manage it properly, you get a new manager who can. There is no need for elaborate controls in the budget process. Too many organizations over control, which is more costly in the long run.

In using long-range planning/MBO, we should not confine the handling of the everyday, regular problems to the short term. We will use this decision model for problem analysis. This decision model should not be confused with the overall planning process. With the strategic plan in mind, a manager uses this outline to systematically solve problems and make short-term decisions. You might want to use this model as you manage your real estate company, for example, to analyze the problem of high turnover of real estate salespeople. You could also use it for other problems such as an overdrawn bank account or a poor cash flow. It is important to use this problem-solving model within the context of the overall strategic planning process. Problems are easier to determine if an organization knows where it is going. I always make sure the group considers purpose, what is going on at the time, strengths and weaknesses, assumptions, objectives, and strategy to set the stage for problem identification.

1.   Defining the problem

2.   Analyzing the problem

3.   Developing alternative solutions

4.   Considering the effect each alternative solution will have on:

   a.   Finance
   b.   Accounting
   c.   Marketing
   d.   Management

5.   Deciding on the best solution

6.   Converting decisions into effective actions. What you are going to do and when?

An example of the outlining format using the decision model follows:

I.   Defining the problem

   A.   Labor turnover too high

II.   Analyzing the problem

   A.   High anxiety

      1.   Poor indoctrination

      2.   Lack of training

   B.   Low pay

III. Developing alternative solutions

   A.   Indoctrination program

      1.   Welcome speech

      2.   Written booklets

      3.   Films

      4.   Training

   B.   Raise commissions of sales to community average

    C.   Keep hiring to cover turnover

        1. Little loyalty

        2. Bad reputation in community

IV.   Deciding on the best solution(s)

    A.   Note choice "X" and "B"

V.   Converting decisions into effective actions

    A.   Convert storeroom to lounge by October 1, 1991

    B.   Buy training film by November 1, 1991

    C.   Develop booklets covering benefits, insurance, etc. by October1, 1991, review rough draft by September 1, 1991

    D.   Train the trainers on each job, training session September-October 8, 1991

    E.   Budget 1-week break-in period on job.

Note further discussion of this problem-solving approach in chapter 10, Strategic Management.

Think of one highly important problem facing you. Follow the outline suggested to determine a tentative solution, and as an exercise, develop a tentative decision using the model.

The use of PERT is another tool that is used in the five-year, or operational, plan. A PERT schedule is an excellent way to implement a strategy to achieve some overall objective. PERT is used in project-oriented or building-related projects (Richards and Nielander, 1974).

Operational planning is what you are going to do in each year, no results, no strategy, no thinking, just doing! Remember that the short-range plan is the first year of the five-year plan. This is what you are doing to implement the strategy to achieve the objectives set previously. Look at one of your objectives and the strategy determined to meet that objective. Now determine exactly what must be done to implement the plan. For example, the objective of the Northeastern State University College of Business might be to have 125 MBAs in the 1990-91 class. The strategy to attain that objective might be to concentrate on the recruiting of NSU seniors, both business and nonbusiness graduates. To implement this strategy, NSU might (1) *develop* a special brochure, (2) *meet* with Admissions, (3) *announce* in class, and 4) *award* scholarships to 3.5 students. Note the action words in italics.

Note that in the five-year plan lower organizational units pick up these operational tasks and reword them as objectives.

Brasfield Construction Company of Jackson, Tennessee, developed a comprehensive strategic plan. They followed the exact outline in the book. All of the managers of Brasfield Construction took part in the planning. After the total plan was agreed upon each manager developed a support plan. Note the format they agreed upon for each construction job. Also note on the bottom of the form where those involved "sign off" on the agreement.

JOB GOALS

JOB DESCRIPTION: _____   JOB# _____

	Estimated Job Costs	Actual Job Costs
Labor	_____	_____
Material	_____	_____
Subcontractors	_____	_____
Other	_____	_____
TOTAL COSTS	_____	_____
Contract Amount	_____	_____

	GOAL	ACTUAL
1. Increased Profit Goal	_____	_____
2. Labor Saving Goal	_____	_____
3. Bonus Goal	_____	_____
4. Job Schedule Improvement Goal	_____	_____

OTHER OBJECTIVES

1. Complete buy out of job and computer estimate input within two weeks of contract.
2. Develop job schedule with superintendent and subcontractors participation.
3. Monitor schedule and adjust with superintendent.
4. Preconstruction conference with men and subcontractors.
5. Annual sales goal of ($_____). Sales goal for personally identified job ($).
6. Develop new contacts (   ) per month.

_____

_____

It is important to have any work group or individual have a voice in determining how their work is to be measured. The Brasfield Construction Job Goals is a good example. It is equally important that goals and performance be revised periodically. Ken Brasfield, president of Brasfield Construction, has developed a very generous reward system if the goals are met.

Examples of Strategy

All organizations are faced with strategic choices. They include: hiring full time vs. temporary workers, length of time to pay bills, whether or not to use alliances, partnerships, mergers or acquisitions, centralize or decentralize, pricing of goods and services. Other examples of strategy include:

Restaurants
1. Expand or cut back menu
2. Provide a drive-in or pick-up service
3. Start catering division

Airlines
1. Raise or lower airfare
2. Senior and/or children discounts
3. Free ticket if flight late

Sports Teams
1. Special attractions, give-away promotions
2. Season ticket packages
3. Starting time of games

University
1. Programs offered
2. Decision to go into adult non-credit courses
3. Research or teaching enrollment

Hotel
4. Free local phone calls
1. Breakfast and/or happy hour included in room ratet

Procter and Gamle
1. Cutting back choices and sizes of detergents, disposable diapers, bathroom tissues, and other household items

Ruffin Properties
1. Converted Galleria Shopping Mall to office complex

NCAA Athletics
1. University of Oklahoma replacing turf with grass

Soft Drinks
1. Pepsi relying on Ray Charles promotions
2. Coke strategy was signing up fast food chains

University/Colleges
1. Oklahoma City University started a lock-step one year MBA program in Tulsa.
2. Northeastern State University added a master in technology program at UCT in Tulsa.

References

Austin, Allen. *Research Report*. New York: American Management Association.

Business Week. "The New Sears," 16 November 1981:140-146.

Carter, Jimmy. "Jimmy Carter Tells Why He Will Use Zero-Base Budgeting". *Nation's Business*. January 1977:24.

Drucker, Peter. *Management*. New York: Harper & Row. 1974.

Hanna. "Marketing Strategy Under Conditions of Economic Scarcity". *Journal of Marketing*. (39-1). 1975:63-67.

Hutchinson, J.G. Readings in Management Strategy and Tactics. Holt McDougal 1971: No. 6, 7.

Pyhrr, Peter. *Zero-Base Budgeting*. New York: John Wiley & Sons. 1973:xi.

Richards, M.D. and Nielander, W.A.. *Readings in Management*. Reading No. 23. South-Western Publishing Co. 1974: 234-235.

Wall Street Journal. "Pricing of Products is Still an Art," 21 November 1981:25.

Wiest, Jerome D. and Ferdinand K. Levy. *A Management Guide to PERT/CPM*. Englewood Cliffs: Prentice-Hall. 1969.

CHAPTER 5
INTEGRATING THE FUNCTIONAL MARKETING PLAN WITH THE CORPORATE STRATEGIC PLAN

A problem that appears to persist in planning environments is the failure to integrate the functional plans with the strategic plan. Such a failure reduces the effectiveness of the planning effort and is counterproductive to the whole planning process.

At the root of this failure is a lack of understanding of the planning hierarchy that integrates the functional plans with the strategic plan. This chapter addresses these issues by providing a clear explanation of the marketing planning process and presents a hierarchical model which focuses on the integration of functional/strategic plans.

Functional Plans

After all members of the top management team have worked on and contributed to the overall plan, it is time to work on functional plans and to get input from marketing, finance, production, research and development, human resources, etc. After the general draft of overall strategic direction is developed, it is time for each functional area to study and give advice on the overall plan. This is called a *time-out period*.

Time-Out Period

Before any plan goes into action, it is important for the whole organization to look it over. It supports the old adage that those who execute the plan need to be in on the plan. This time-out period helps eliminate mistakes. Top management of any organization cannot possibly know all details, opportunities, and problems. There is talent in all organizations, and the time-out period gives the organizations a chance to use that talent and to listen. Too often plans are made and announced with little or no input. The time-out period helps assure that people will support the plan. You can guarantee apathy and little support if the strategic direction is set with no input.

Personnel in each functional area, production, marketing, etc. discuss the overall plan and submit a written critique in a four- to six-week period. Then top management get together and rethink each step in the overall plan. Adjustments are made and an overall plan is set.

Strategic Plans

In review, strategic planning is the philosophy of managing with a planning process. It is both a product and a process. The product is the plan itself. It is in writing and clearly defines where the organization intends to be in the long term, usually three or more years in the future. The plan includes strategy and the short-term steps to ensure overall success. The process is the interaction that takes place in developing the plan. Everyone involved in executing the plan should be involved in its development.

Functional plans are the strategic plans developed to support the overall corporate strategic plan. Functional plans include manufacturing, personnel, research and development, marketing, and finance. They are basically the same philosophy and process described in chapter 1.

In review, the firm must establish its overall long-term strategic plan first. The essence of this plan is determining where the organization wants to be five to ten years in the future and mobilizing its resources to get there. Recall that the top management team must meet and work together through the following steps:

1. Defining the organization's purpose and reason for being

2. Monitoring the environment in which it operates

3. Realistically assessing strengths and weaknesses

4. Making assumptions about unpredictable future events

5. Prescribing written, specific, and measurable objectives in principal result areas contributing to the purpose

6. Developing strategies on how to use available resources to meet objectives

7. Constantly appraising performance to determine whether it is keeping pace with attainment of objectives and is consistent with defined purpose

8. Reevaluating purpose, environment, strengths, weaknesses, assumptions, objectives, and strategies before setting objectives for the next performance year.

The strategic planning and management process should be viewed as a continuing, ongoing, orderly process. It is cybernetic in nature as developed in Chapter 1 and presented again in Figure 5-1. The top management team works together developing Steps 1 through 7. The overall direction of the organization is determined, usually focusing on five years, but with a view toward the future. Figure 5-1 demonstrates the overall planning process.

Figure 5-1

Strategic Long-Range Planning Process

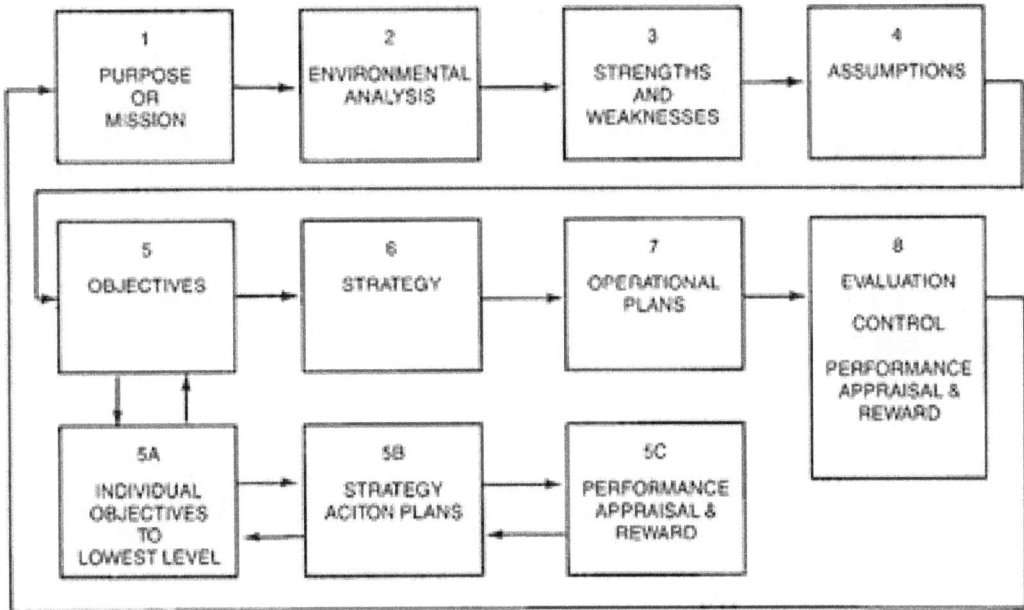

The strategic planning process should be viewed as a flexible, dynamic, and continuous process that assumes a democratic or participative style of management. It integrates various plans by providing appropriate linkage between short- and long-term plans. Its purpose is to allocate scarce resources in order to ensure continuous achievement.

Once the overall direction of the firm has been determined, then each functional area must develop a functional plan to support the overall strategic plan. These support plans include, for example, the marketing plan, human resources plan, financial plan, R&D plan, and production plan. Note Figure 5-2 demonstrates the relationship between the overall plan and the functional plan.

Figure 5-2.

Overall Strategic Plan

Too often, each functional entity works to develop its own plan without coordinating with other areas. In those situations, one functional area plan, like marketing, may tend to dominate the planning process.

To avoid this, all members of the top management team need to develop the overall plan that best meets the needs of the firm and keep it striving to serve its mission and purpose statement. This is the benchmark plan. The marketing plan should not be developed until the marketing management team can see the overall direction of the firm and how the marketing plan fits with other functional area plans. The marketing manager should participate in the overall planning of the firm to ensure the integration of the marketing plan with the strategic plan.

For example, the company might decide to be an international supplier of widgets. It wants to grow to a certain sales and profit position and be a leader in the international marketplace. With this in mind, the optimum production plan might call for production facilities near the customer. Service and fast delivery might be considered as keys to the marketing plan. This results in higher manufacturing costs, but lower transportation costs. The optimum-size plan must be developed to serve each of the individual markets. In some market areas it might be cheaper to supply the market from a central plant, pay higher transportation costs, and let the market develop. Capital budgeting decisions must be made to ensure the right plant and equipment are at the right spot to maximize profitability. None of these functional area decisions should be made without a full view of the strategic direction of the business.

An example of how complex and forward-thinking marketing/production strategy must be comes from the motorcycle industry. The normal view is to look at a least-cost manufacturing alternative. Standardize everything, make few changes, build to plant capacity, and try to optimize the plant capacity at the bottom of the long-run average cost curve. This produces a least-cost manufacturing product, in this case, motorcycles, motorcycle engines, and parts. However, standardization contributes to replacement by competition. It allows entry by other firms into the lucrative replacement parts and repair business. The Japanese constantly redesign, remodel, and change after shorter production runs to discourage this kind of competition. Even though the engineering research and short-term production costs are higher, the long-term overall profits to the firm are maximized.

The Japanese .change their oil filter design every year on their engines to keep the big oil filter makers out of the replacement parts business. The money to be made in motorcycles, as in so many other products, is with the replacement parts market. This is not necessarily the best strategy in all types of business. The main point here is to emphasize the fact that top management must look at the long-term potential of the firm, recognizing the characteristics in the marketplace and the overall long-term best return on assets for the organization. The emphasis should be to look at the total picture and make the functional plans fit neatly into the overall plan of the firm. The emphasis must be on the firm and maximizing the achievement of all the firm's specific measurable objectives.

Marketing Planning

Nowhere in the organization is planning more needed than in marketing. The complexity of today's environment in terms of social, legal, environmental, economic, competitive, and resource constraints requires a high degree of skill to provide structure to a course of action an organization can follow to achieve desired results.

For the marketing managers, the marketing planning process becomes paramount. The marketing concept or philosophy has its major impact on an organization's operating procedures when it is reflected in the performance of the administrative function of planning. The customer's needs are the focus of an organization's operations under the marketing philosophy, and this can be paramount in the planning process. Which customer segments will the organization try to serve? How will the marketing functions be performed? Who will perform them? What sales volume will be generated? These are all questions which are answered by a well-thought-out and carefully written marketing plan. In essence, the plan becomes a tool through which the marketing concept is implemented into the decision-making procedures.

The marketing plan does not necessarily differ in format from the strategic plan. In fact, it must cover some of the same basic topics, objectives, strategies, and so forth. The difference is in scope and time frame. The corporate plan is broad in scope and may lay out a strategy which is never departed from if successful. The strategic marketing plan focuses on the marketing decisions needed to support the overall plan. This is then used to develop the operating plan. This plan is a short-run plan and normally coincides with the organization's fiscal year. The operating plan deals only with the current operating environment and specifically addresses only important events that influence changes in the detailed tactical decisions in such areas as advertising themes, product changes, etc. The marketing plan, whether strategic or operational, is a written document which contains seven basic elements: (1) purpose of talent, (2) a summary of the environmental analysis, including general developments, consumer analysis, competitive analysis, and opportunity analysis, (3) strengths and weaknesses, (4) a set of objectives, (5) a detailed strategy statement of how the marketing variables will be combined to achieve those objectives as well as the financial impact of the strategy, (6) sales management plan, (7) performance appraisal, (8) a set of procedures for monitoring, and controlling the plan through feedback of results. An outline of the format for a marketing plan is shown in Table 1.

Table 1: Outline of a Marketing Plan

I.   Purpose of marketing

II.   Environmental analysis

    A. Market analysis

    B. Customer analysis

    C. Competitive analysis

    D. Opportunity analysis

III.   Strengths and weaknesses

IV.   Objectives

    A. Sales objectives

    B. Profitability objectives

    C. Customer objectives

V.   Strategy

    A. Overall strategy

    B. Marketing mix variables

    C. Financial impact statement

VI.   Marketing operating/sales management plan

VII.   Performance appraisal

VIII.   Keeping the marketing plan on target

The logic of this approach to planning is clear:

We must (1) determine where we are now, (environmental analysis), (2) decide where we want to go (objectives), (3) decide how we are going to get there (strategy), and (4) decide what feedback we need to let us know if we are keeping on course (performance appraisal). A well-designed marketing plan provides the answers to these questions.

The feasibility of combining products together for planning purposes depends on the similarities of the needs of customers and the similarities of the marketing variables required to meet their needs. For example, a firm may develop a plan for a whole line of products aimed at the same customers. Frigidaire has used this approach with its line of appliances and the theme "I should have bought a Frigidaire.

Integrating Corporate and Functional Plans

For planning to produce optimum results, there must be an interrelationship established in the plans developed at the corporate, business, functional, and operational levels. The logical flow of such plans is depicted in Figure 5-3. The corporate mission determines the appropriate corporate objectives. The corporate strategy is then developed to accomplish these objectives. If there are several strategic business units, each should develop a strategic plan including a mission statement, objectives, and strategy. These are referred to as business level because they relate to a specific SBU.

With most companies, a single set of overall objectives does not provide sufficient detail for operating management. Rather there is a hierarchy of objectives which reflects the specificity of the contribution of the part to the whole. In other words, overall corporate objectives would be expected to be more general in nature than business level ones. Business level objectives, in turn, would be more general than functional area objectives. The greater the degree to which the contribution of a department, product group, or product can be specified, the more specific the objectives.

Although objectives may originate anywhere in the organization, the most logical sequence is to start at the top and flow down to lower levels in the structure. Knowledge of and alignment with this hierarchy is mandatory to integrate the total organization by fostering commonality of purpose and unity in decision making.

In most planning scenarios, strategy follows objectives. Thus the development of the corporate strategy follows the identification of corporate objectives. Just as there is a hierarchy of objectives which flows from corporate to functional to operational, there is also a hierarchy of strategies. Strategies in the functional areas (marketing, production, and finance) must support the overall corporate strategy.

The functional marketing plan, along with plans for other functional areas, must be developed to support the business level strategy. It is the strategic plan for the functional area. The operating marketing plan is then developed as the short-run plan which details the tactical decisions in the marketing area for the operational planning period, usually a year.

Figure 5-3
The Organizational Hierarchy of Objectives and Strategies

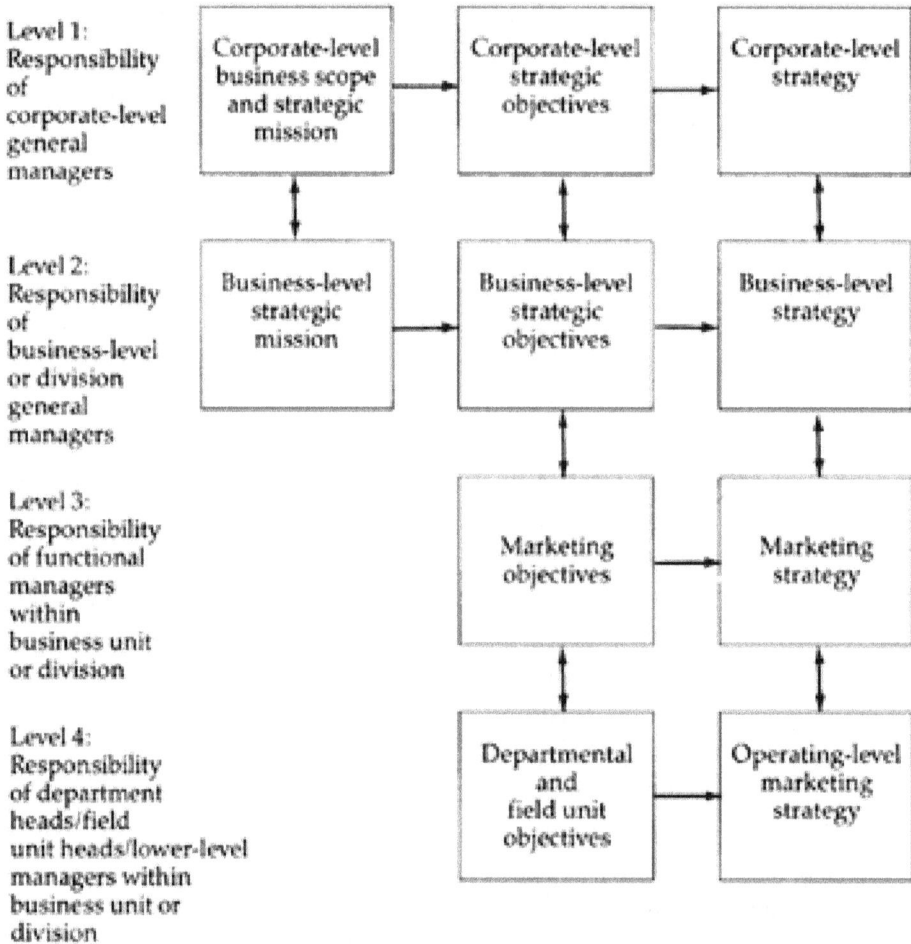

Level 1: Responsibility of corporate-level general managers	Corporate-level business scope and strategic mission	Corporate-level strategic objectives	Corporate-level strategy
Level 2: Responsibility of business-level or division general managers	Business-level strategic mission	Business-level strategic objectives	Business-level strategy
Level 3: Responsibility of functional managers within business unit or division		Marketing objectives	Marketing strategy
Level 4: Responsibility of department heads/field unit heads/lower-level managers within business unit or division		Departmental and field unit objectives	Operating-level marketing strategy

Source: Adapted from Arthur A. Thompson, Jr. and A.J. Strickland III, *Strategy Formulation and Implementation*, Third Edition, Business Publications, Inc., Plano, Texas, 1986, p. 58.

The interrelationship that should exist in this planning hierarchy is demonstrated in Figure 5-4. This figure shows the corporate, business, functional, and operating strategies for a movie theater chain. Note the flow from corporate to operating strategy. Each strategy is developed to support the strategy at the next highest level. However, the strategy development flows from top to bottom, i.e. the corporate strategy must be established first so that the business level strategy can be developed to support the corporate strategy. This flow continues down to the lowest level of planning in the firm, the operating level.

Figure 5-4

Integration of Strategies for a Movie Chain

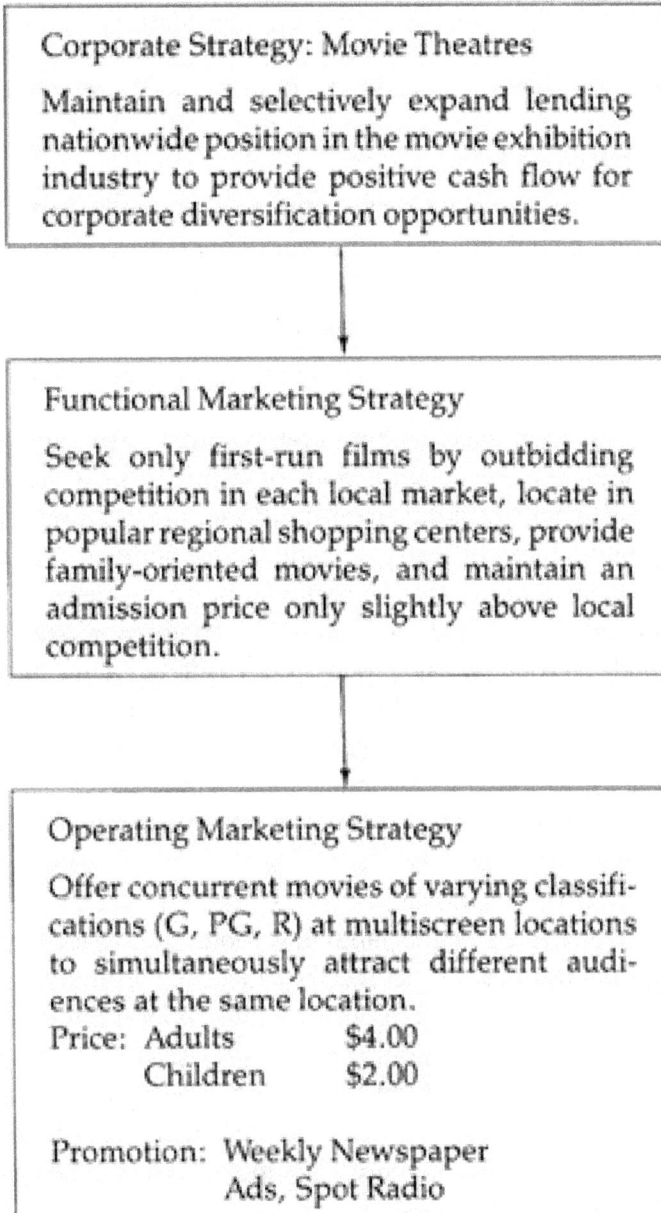

Corporate Strategy: Movie Theatres

Maintain and selectively expand lending nationwide position in the movie exhibition industry to provide positive cash flow for corporate diversification opportunities.

Functional Marketing Strategy

Seek only first-run films by outbidding competition in each local market, locate in popular regional shopping centers, provide family-oriented movies, and maintain an admission price only slightly above local competition.

Operating Marketing Strategy

Offer concurrent movies of varying classifications (G, PG, R) at multiscreen locations to simultaneously attract different audiences at the same location.

Price: Adults $4.00
       Children $2.00

Promotion: Weekly Newspaper
            Ads, Spot Radio

The corporate strategy is to grow through diversification from cash provided from the movie division of the company. The marketing strategy focuses on generating cash flow through showing first-run movies at multiscreen locations to generate the volume needed for profitable levels of operations.

The operating strategy is more specific and even specifies current prices and promotional plans. These short-term aspects of the operational plan may change several times during the year based on competitive moves, special matinées, or promotions. The lower price for children reflects the strategic orientation toward families.

There must be alignment of the functional and operational strategy with the corporate strategy. This assures consistency in the functional areas to support the overall corporate strategy in achieving organizational objectives.

Sales Management Plan

Everyone involved in executing the plan needs to be in on the plan. Cross Manufacturing brought all their sales and marketing representatives into Kansas City recently in order to get firsthand input on helping develop the marketing plan. That set the stage to develop the sales plan. The sales plan includes sales force organization, selection, training, motivation, compensation, and evaluation.

If you are involved in business on an international level, are you spending enough time drinking mint tea, playing polo, or sailing in the Riviera? According to expert business managers, time spent in developing a strong understanding of cultural norms and in cultivating relationships built on mutual trust and acceptance is of the essence in the international business scene.

T. D. Williamson, Inc. (TOW), a Tulsa-based international firm serving the pipeline and petrochemical processing plant segment of the energy industry, conducts 55 percent of its business outside the United States and is a proven example of how corporate strategies successfully deal with vast cultural differences. Employing a sophisticated strategic long-range planning process, each level of TOW's management works conjunctively with the levels immediately above and below to synchronize the agreed-upon objectives and strategies. When the top functional managers from all over the world convene annually to discuss the strategies and new objectives based on strengths, weaknesses, and environmental factors, they discover profitable opportunities and dedicate a long-term effort to capitalize on those opportunities. For example, during the past year, TOW has emphasized the strategy of maximizing its worldwide production capabilities by selectively placing orders in the factory having available capacity, but not necessarily the regular source of supply. The customer will accept an alternate source of supply, provided he has confidence and trust in the individual with whom primary contact is maintained, preferably a national.

This is good planning and simply good management, true, but unless the corporate plans are carefully adapted to the individual foreign segments based on local custom, the company's options are reduced. In this particular case, an order to a foreign customer was moved from a United States manufacturing plant to a TDW plant in Belgium. The TDW Belgium plant is not running at capacity, and it is against the social fabric to lay off workers in Belgium as it is in the United States. Recognizing this, the order was placed in Belgium.

TDW managers have found that the key difference in strategic planning for foreign operations is the perspective time. In most countries it is essential to spend enormous amounts of time establishing personal relationships, building trust. This is where TDW does its homework. "You can't go into a foreign country with preconceived ideas. You have to play by their rules, use their methods to accomplish the ultimate objectives. If you don't, you'll get heavy resistance and probably failure, a TDW executive commented. He cited one instance in which he learned this lesson the hard way when he was setting up the company's operation in France. The home office wanted increased sales from particular key accounts, and the strategy was to take a typically American, aggressive approach to convince these clients of their need for TDW's equipment through seminars. After numerous frustrating attempts to build up these accounts, the French sales manager suggested a more relaxed approach, one in which personal relationships could be established through long lunches and participation in local social activities. Convinced there was a better way, top management moved the operation closer to the location of the key account companies. For a year the sales manager demonstrated to his clients his willingness to listen to their complaints and to participate in their pastimes, with satisfactory results. Trust was soon established between the two companies and sales for TDW began to soar.

TDW's manager of customer service commented that the same principles apply to the Middle East countries, which he says will continue to be the "hot spot" for American international business for many years to come. It is, therefore, vital that American business people understand the Arab culture and how the differences affect business management in those countries. "They need us and we need them. They need our engineering ability and we need their energy resources."

In Saudi Arabia, where the pace is much slower than in the United States, business executives must learn to like drinking hot mint tea. This not an option. It is customary, and to refuse this form of Arab hospitality is a grave insult.

Also, to understand Islam, the religion of the Middle East, is to understand the law. Their religion is tied to everything. There is also a strong emphasis on family relationships. Because of Western dominance, the only stability they really know stems from family connections. This means that in order to be successful in these countries, a management team must first recognize the power structure, learn who calls the shots, and establish a local contact base, usually a family enterprise and often tied to a government power. These are the threads of commonality weaving throughout the Muslim countries.

Generally speaking, most Arabs are very capable businessmen. Females do not participate in social or business activities; therefore, to send a woman in a management capacity to one of these areas would be unthinkable. They love to bargain, and in negotiations they will never accept the first offer. Arabs just don't consider a transaction a bargain unless they have spent long, grueling hours haggling over it.

These extremely proud, emotional, and expressive people may have little concern for time, but they do place a high premium on integrity, trust, and service after the sale. A TDW executive remarks of the Arab businessman, "If you stick to the same facts without wavering, you'll keep his business, but he will always be checking you out, scrutinizing everything."

There is usually a good reason why a local custom differs from yours, if you only take the time to find out the background.

It has become apparent to the authors that for American businesses to successfully enter foreign regions, they must take time, *lots of it,* to understand the many cultural differences, and adjust their strategies to the difference in the perspective of time itself. This puts a new twist to the American adage, "Time is money."

This same advice holds true for North American businesses. Relationships must be established with the people you do business with. More emphasis in serving and helping, and less "selling" is important.

Keys to Successful Selling

The key to the sales management plan is service. The old "hype-up-the-sales-force" and "the martini lunch" days are over. Customers are becoming increasingly knowledgeable and sophisticated in their dealings with suppliers. Sales people should do their homework in their area before ever making a call. The first meeting with a client should be to get acquainted.

What are the needs of the customer? What problems is he having? What can the selling company do to improve product and/or service? Then follow-up like a bulldog. Increased sales start taking care of themselves.

Summary

This chapter has emphasized the importance of integrating the marketing plan with the overall strategic plan for an organization. Failure to integrate the functional plans with the business level and corporate plan will result in lower optimization in planning and reduce the likelihood of successfully achieving corporate objectives. In turn, such a failure can result in constant conflicts among functional managers as each strives to position his own plan as the driving force in the company.

As a reminder, objectives can be set in the following areas:

Sales

> Total sales
> Net sales per dollar of net worth
> Net sales per dollar of total assets
> Net sales per dollar of net working capital
> Cost of sales per dollar of inventory
> Net sales per dollar of depreciated fixed assets

Market Potential

> Percent regional market share
> Percent national market share
> Percent world market share
> Percent products in introductory stage
> Percent products in maturity stage
> Percent products in declining stage

Marketing Research

> Usually on a project basis
> Objectives set on every project

Sales Management

> Revenue per territory
> Quotas/objectives for sales teams
> Quotas/objectives per person

The Marketing Plan Must Address These Questions:

> Where do products fit product life cycle?
> How do products fit performance/potential matrix?
> What is optimum product mix?
> What is present contribution to profit per product line?
> What is expected contribution to profit per product in 1995?
> What products should be added to present product mix?
> What products should be dropped from present product mix?

How do you react to a rapidly changing marketplace?

What opportunities are available due to changes in Russia, Europe, and the Pacific Rim, etc.?

Contemporary Marketing

What goes around comes around.

James O. McKinsey in the early 1920s used a creative strategy to get to know his customers. McKinsey throughout his career used the business lunch as an effective marketing tool. He scheduled lunches with a wide range of community leaders. The lunches were not restricted to just business leaders and customers. He got to know education, clergy, government and community leaders. There was no sales pitch. He didn't try to sell anything. He wanted to know how they felt about different issues. He was interested in their plans and problems.

Today McKinsey is one of the worlds most respected international consulting companies.

Marketing and sales for years seemed to center around developing a product and selling it to a customer. My roommate back in my single days was an IBM salesman. I recall in the evenings he would practice his "sales pitch." His presentation was polished, the handouts and support material were as expected, "Big Blue" quality.

The science and art of closing the sale remains today an intriguing process. From my perspective organizations worldwide used this process for selling their products. Guess what? The "new" trend in marketing is called customer oriented selling by IBM, and Xerox Canada called it solution selling. The "new" concept calls for going to the customer, finding out about future plans, problems, and products. The marketing manager in this last decade of the century has learned to be customer focused.

The key is to find out how your organization can help the customer solve problems, gain market share and be more profitable. With the information gathered, you go back and put together a multilevel, multidiscipline task force to see what specific products, services, and solutions your company can come up with. This is not a "let's adapt what we have and see if it will fit approach." It is a creative, innovative look at the customer and perceived needs.

The "solution" might mean a capital investment. It could require a complete change in what you considered time honored policy and procedure.

Your customer is eager to have the follow-up meeting. There is a keen interest in finding out what you have to offer.

This customer focus, whether you call it customer oriented selling or solution selling becomes one of the ways you differentiate your company from your competitor. You don't want selling price to be the only criteria your customers can judge you by.

The trend I see over the past few years is for customers and suppliers working together strategically for a common good. When I grew up working for my father in a Western Auto Store in Collinsville, Oklahoma, I recall one of his favorite themes "a good business deal is one that benefits both parties." Every organization that adds value to the product and/or service must receive a fair reward for their labor. There is a Biblical principle that states "A man is worthy of his hire."

The Three Reasons We Are Here

To keep existing customers

To create new customers

To make ourselves and our organization the kind that people want to do business with.

References

Migliore, R. Henry and Walt Thrun. *Production and Operations Management: A Productivity Approach*. New Jersey: G P Publishing, 1990.

CHAPTER 6
PRODUCTION/OPERATIONS MANAGEMENT OF THE STRATEGIC LONG-RANGE PLAN

This chapter establishes the importance of the production-management plan and key operations officers in the development of the overall strategic long-range plan for an organization. Over the past 20 years, most strategic plans have been either inspired by marketing or financing. Little attention has been paid to the production process

Also stressed is the importance of the systems approach in coordinating the production plan with other functional plans as they support the overall strategic plan.

The objectives of the chapter are to: (1) understand the concept of strategic planning for the firm, (2) see how the production manager fits into the overall planning process, (3) shoe how the production plan contributes to the overall strategic plan, (4) explain why the production plan is important and necessary, and (5) introduce the systems approach to the production process.

The production plan cannot be made unless the production management team can see the overall direction of the firm and how the production plan must fit the financial and marketing plans. The production manager must participate in the overall planning for the firm.

In my first planning responsibility as chief industrial engineer of a Continental Can Company, Inc. manufacturing plant in the mid-1960s, we went through the typical process. Everything started with a marketing forecast and then all other parts of the organization adapted their planning process to the marketing plan. This is absolutely the wrong approach. The marketing plan often can't recognize the financial implications, and most certainly has little insight into the production implications of some of its decisions. I learned that lesson as manager of press manufacturing at another Continental plant two years later.

As I drove down the Dan Ryan Expressway one morning, I heard an unusual "easy open" can being advertised for an automobile product. I remember thinking: "I'm glad I'm not in his production manager's shoes." Later that week my boss informed me that R&D was coming in to start adapting equipment and running experiments for developing the new "easy open" can for an automobile product. Clearly production and research were not involved in any of the planning. The product was advertised to be on the shelf in a big Memorial Day campaign. Independence Day found the top research and engineering people in the company assembled in Chicago trying to figure out why the manufacturing process wasn't working properly. Poor planning, marketing dominance, and lack of input had created a monstrous situation.

A company might decide to be an international supplier of widgets. It wants to grow to a certain sales and profit position and be a leader in the international marketplace. With this in mind, the optimum production plan might call for production facilities near the customer. Service and fast delivery could have been determined as a key to the marketing plan. This results in higher manufacturing costs but lower transportation costs. The optimum size plant must be developed to serve each of the individual markets. In some market areas it might be cheaper to supply the market from a central plant, pay higher transportation costs, and let the market develop. Capital budgeting decisions must be made to ensure the right plant and that equipment is at the right spot to maximize profitability. None of these decisions can be made without a full view of the business.

Recall the example in the previous chapter from the motorcycle industry. A least-cost manufacturing alternative can have an adverse effect on the company. Standardize everything, make few changes, build to plant capacity, and try to optimize the plant capacity at the bottom of the long-run average cost curve. This produces a least-cost manufacturing product, in this case motorcycles, motorcycle engines, and parts. However, standardization contributes to replacement by competition. It allows entry by other firms into the lucrative replacement cost and repair business. The Japanese constantly redesign, remodel, and change after shorter production runs to discourage this kind of competition. Even though the engineering, research, and short-term production costs are higher, the long-term, overall profits to the firm are maximized. Many manufacturing executives have trouble with their strategies. I know I did early in my career with Continental Can. In that era, I don't believe any of us in manufacturing felt like we were part of the team. We fought for long runs and few changeovers.

Recall that the Japanese change their oil filter design every year on their engines to keep the big oil filter makers out of the replacement-part business. The money to be made in motorcycles, as in so many other products, is with the replacement-parts market. This is not necessarily the best strategy in all types of business. The main point here is to emphasize that top management must look at the long-term potential of the firm, recognizing the characteristics in the marketplace and the overall long-term best return on assets for the organization. Too often in our experience we rush into production and operations design, manufacturing, and quality problems using traditional approaches. The emphasis is to look at the total picture and to make the production operations plan fit neatly into the overall plan of the firm. The emphasis must be on the firm and maximizing the achievement of all of the firm's specific measurable objectives.

The eighth and ninth steps in the strategic planning process implicitly state that a firm operates as a system. Consider that a system basically is an array of components designed to accomplish a particular objective according to plan.

As the strategic plan is the expression of the firm's reason for being, so the goods and services are the expression of the strategic plan. How many types of firms or business entities exist without producing goods or providing services? Strategic plans are expressed in terms of goods and services. Examples:

1. Capture a 25 percent share of the world market for widgets in three years.

2. Develop substitute composite materials to replace aluminum in commercial aircraft within five years.

3. Operate a motel chain at 85 percent occupancy level for next three years.

4. Enter the hydraulic valve market within two years.

5. Employ wide-body jets in transpacific flights before Braniff is revived.

A very obvious void exists between the firm's strategic plan and the "goods and services" segment. The implementation of the strategic plan is missing. The missing segment is the firm's production plan! A firm need not be a manufacturer to have a production plan. Let's reconsider the aforementioned five examples of strategic planning items.

1. The firm desiring a 25 percent share of the widget market may not be a manufacturer at all; it may be a distributor for several brands of widgets. If in fact the firm is in the distribution end of the business, the production plan might well involve transportation and storage facilities.

2. Strategy to develop substitute composite materials for aluminum might be an aircraft manufacturer, an engineering firm, the D.O.D., or a university research department. Once again, the gathering of resources to meet the strategic plan is the production plan.

3. The objective to operate a motel chain at a given occupancy rate requires a production plan to provide for energy, maintenance help, cleaning service, and many other related services.

4. The strategy to enter the hydraulic-valve market could be for a manufacturer of completed products, say pumps, or a supplier of component parts such as a foundry which would cast the valve body itself. In either case, the production plan would involve manufacturing

processes, equipment and tooling acquisition, training of the labor force, provisions for raw material, etc.

5.   The strategy to employ wide-body jets in its service would most likely be for a commercial airline. The production plan would involve providing for larger staging areas at the airports to be served, additional sanitation disposal service, and additional cabin service among other things.

The above five items all have one very basic thing in common. They all represent portions of a firm's strategic plan which are accomplished by means of the production plan. Without proper input from operations executives, it would be difficult for the organization to achieve its purpose.

It can be confidently stated that all strategic plans are implemented and/or achieved via the production of goods and/or services.

The production plan, therefore, is perhaps the most important segment of the total system representing a firm or business entity. A production plan exists whenever a strategic plan exists.

The absence of a formal production planning process results in an informal system in which companies inefficiently react to situations rather than taking well-coordinated and thought-out steps in anticipation of events.

In manufacturing environments, the production control function should play a vital role in the process of developing strategies and goals that will support the implementation of the production plan. However, a great majority of companies today still fail to use a formal system that could generate information to develop plans that other people could be held accountable for executing. This results in production planning and control becoming just an order launching and expediting function. This area generates orders, puts due dates on them, and then the expediting system tries to determine what material is really needed and when. This reacting mode creates an atmosphere of distrust, and many persons become dissatisfied because of their inability to work effectively.

A case in point is a small manufacturing plant in the southwest that produces a variety of highly engineered products for the process-control industry. No formal planning process existed. Marketing, engineering, and manufacturing all recognized that costs were excessive, inventories inflated, and that the customer was not receiving the kind of service that would keep this company competitive in the marketplace. This cycle was never ending, beginning at the first of each month, and culminating with the month end rush that ineffectively tried to meet demand.

In an effort to resolve this problem, general management instigated a "production meeting." Representatives from marketing, engineering, accounting, production planning and control, and manufacturing were required to sit down four times a week for approximately two hours. These were middle management personnel whose sole objective was to generate daily action steps that would end their inability to meet marketplace requirements.

Upper management ultimately recognized that this daily production meeting was not a substitute for a formal planning process. Management addressed the problem and developed a planning process that would provide the necessary information and decision-making capabilities to effectively operate the business. This process became so effective that the daily production meeting became almost obsolete. The meeting is now held on a once-a-month basis in which each area is responsible for reviewing performances and contributing to the modification of future plans.

Objectives, strategies, and action plans must be set for equipment overhaul, preventive maintenance, check maintenance, and running maintenance.

An army travels on its stomach. A manufacturing company travels on its machinery. Good sound maintenance programs pay off in the long run. A manufacturing company either acts or reacts. It acts with sound maintenance, cleanup, and lubrication. It reacts if it just runs equipment until there is a breakdown.

Chapter 7
Financial Planning and the Organization's Strategic Plan

Financial planning practices vary from very sophisticated, fine-tuned financial planning with a long-range focus, to developing a strategic plan and allowing the financial plan to take care of itself.

In some cases, organizations have financially driven, budget-oriented planning, but mistakenly call this strategic planning. This particular effort does not take into account the overall direction of the firm and its particular strategies in such areas as product mix, pricing, and diversification.

Granted, all organizations plan differently for the future, and, because of many factors such as financial officers, personalities, strengths, and weaknesses, the organization may use those persons differently in plan development.

These observations and experiences, along with a search of the literature, provide the basis for this chapter and a study of financial planning practice of corporations. Also discussed is how the capital budget ties into the financial plan.

Background

The financial implications of either strategy formulation or implementation are often given only a cursory glance or are completely ignored; however, recent environmental changes have forced many CEOs to question the viability, and even feasibility, of their originally developed strategic plans (Malermee and Jaffe, 1985). Malermee and Jaffe offer an integrative approach to strategic and financial planning. The authors give an example of how a company developed a strategic plan with a growth strategy that was impossible because of financial implications. If a financial plan had not been developed, the company would have followed the wrong path and realized its mistake too late after resources had been allocated.

Applications of financial analysis and planning models to strategic management have been discussed by Duhaime and Thomas (1983). They define the concept of strategy and the nature of strategic problems, and then present a useful organizing paradigm of the strategic management field. Against that backdrop, the discussed financial analysis applications, various financial analysis, and planning models are reviewed, focusing on their usefulness to strategic management.

The relationship between formality of planning procedures and financial performance was examined for a sample of small U.S. banks by Robinson and Pearce. They describe how small banks without formal planning systems performed equally with small banks with formal plans. Regardless of formality, each set of banks placed equal emphasis on all aspects of strategic decision making except formalized goals and objectives. Results suggest that managers responsible for strategic planning activities in smaller organizations do not appear to benefit from a highly formalized planning process, extensive written documentation, or the use of mission and goal identification as the beginning of a strategic planning process.

Strategic planning tasks should emphasize the two dimensions of thought (Grawoig and Hubbard, 1982). Decision makers should develop the firm's overall picture. Usually one prepares detailed budgets based on chain reasoning models, such as financial accounting. Such an apparent paradox has led to some half-truths such as: "Models are not much help in solving policy problems." Unless a problem solver conceptualizes the overall system, and unless he employs intuition and creativity, plans will certainly be inadequate if not outright failures.

During the first quarter, the corporate financial planning group should request each profit center to provide its five-year financial plan (Allio and Pennington, 1979). The annual objective should become the first year of the five-year plan. During the second quarter, profit center financial plans should be reviewed, analyzed, and consolidated by the corporate financial planning group, and then presented to top management for review and comments. After necessary revisions are made in line with the overall corporate strategy and management judgment, the long-range financial plan is submitted to the board of directors for approval. The plans are updated for known changes and reviewed by top management and the board of directors each quarter.

The strengths and weaknesses of corporate-strategic planning systems have been reviewed by Allen. In 1979, fewer than 25 percent of respondents indicated that their companies had corporate strategic plans. When the study was repeated again in 1984, more than 75 percent said they had strategic plans. Five years ago, business planning was centered heavily on financial plans and objectives, and was relatively weak in the area of strategic analysis.

A recent study indicates that 48 percent of companies surveyed with over 251 employees had a written strategic plan with defined long-term objectives *(Wall Street Journal,*1986). The study stated: "(1) a large percentage of the respondents did not use a specific financial leverage measure as a constraint on the mix of debt and equity, (2) a majority of the firms did not have a target financial structure that they maintained, and (3) many did not see a relationship between the use of debt financing and the cost of capital. Consistent with earlier cited research, a larger percentage of the large firms utilized the above mentioned concepts" (Lamberson, 1988).

We recently conducted a study to determine actual financial planning practices and opinions of practitioners in the field. The study investigated and then suggested how financial planning can support an organization's overall strategic plan. This chapter suggests how a financial plan should be developed.

Research Methodology

The data gathered and conclusions for the chapter came from three sources: (1) mailed questionnaires, (2) personal interviews with 10 financial officers of major companies, and (3) the author's experience.

The responses to the mailed questionnaires were entered into a machine readable form and computer analyzed using SAS. One-way and two-way frequency tables were generated as well as appropriate statistical tests such as chi-square and t-test. The following subgroups were compared:

A.   Firms with annual planning meetings versus those with more frequent meetings

B.   Firms that have five-year financial objectives versus those not setting five-year financial objectives

C.   Smaller firms ($100 million in sales or less) versus larger firms.

Study I

A total of 78 questionnaires were mailed to members of the Northeastern Oklahoma Financial Executives Institute (Appendix B). The purpose of the study was to determine actual financial planning practices and opinions of practitioners in the field. A total of 38 responded by the cutoff date and their responses were analyzed. Overall results of the study are in Appendix B, and are presented on the questionnaire.

The following 15 conclusions were drawn from the survey responses:

1.   Few organizations (18.4%) do not have regular strategic planning meetings that focus on three to five years.

2.   Of those with long-range strategic planning which focused on three to five years, almost all (96.9%) responded that someone from the finance function is usually at these meetings.

3.   Of those with the finance function being represented at the strategic planning meetings, more than half (54.8%) reported that the finance participant is very active at these meetings.

4. Those firms that had annual planning meetings generally did not set measurable objectives for the break-even point (16.7%), while firms with more frequent meetings did set measurable objectives for the break-even point (60.0%).

5. Those firms with five-year financial objectives almost always set a measurable objective for NPAT on net worth (93.3%), while those not setting five-year financial objectives were much lower (64.3%).

6. Those firms with no five-year financial objectives more frequently set financial objectives for NPAT on net sales (76.9%) than those firms with five-year objectives (42.9%).

7. Smaller firms ($100 million in sales or less) almost always (90.9%) mention current assets/current liabilities as a measurable objective, while larger firms reported more infrequently (61.9%).

8. Larger firms seldom mentioned break-even point (19.1%) as a measurable objective, while smaller firms generally did (70.0%).

9. Capital structure was the most frequently mentioned function within the finance discipline for which measurable objectives were set for five years. Financing cash requirements was second and asset management was third. The most infrequently mentioned objective was foreign exchange exposure.

10. NPAT on net worth was the most frequently mentioned category for which a measurable objective was set. Current assets/current liabilities was second, current and long-term liabilities/Net worth was third, and average collection period was fourth. Net sales/dollar of depreciated fixed assets was the most infrequently mentioned objective.

11. Firms which set five-year measurable objectives for the finance function rated NPAT on net worth (profitability) the most frequently mentioned objective. Those firms without five-year measurable objectives for the finance function mentioned current assets to current liabilities (liquidity) most frequently and NPAT on net worth tied for fourth.

12. Larger firms mentioned NPAT on net worth most frequently, while smaller firms mentioned current assets to current liabilities most frequently.

13. Larger firms generally had annual planning meetings (62.5%), while smaller firms generally met more frequently than one time per year (62.5%).

14. Larger firms generally had five-year measurable objectives for the finance function (57.9%), while smaller companies generally had no five-year measurable objectives (33.3%).

15. In the smaller firms, the finance participant was much more active (75.0%) as compared with larger firms (47.6%).

Study II

A total of 50 questionnaires were mailed out to the 50 largest public corporations in Oklahoma with a total of 24 responding. The purpose of Study II was to follow up and expand on Study I which had been sent only to members of the Oklahoma Financial Executives Institute. The questionnaire was expanded and improved as a result of the information gained from completing Study I. Overall results are in Appendix C.

The following seven major conclusions were drawn from Study II:

1. Most companies set objectives and have these objectives written down (86.4%).

2. Someone from the finance function is at the long-range strategic meeting (88.2%).

3. The finance function generally has measurable objective for one year (85.7%), only approximately half have for three years (50.0%) and five years (45.5%).

4. Examining functions within the finance discipline:

    A. Measurable objectives were always set for capital structure, cash management, and financing cash requirements. Measurable objectives are generally not set for foreign exchange exposure (71.2%).

    B. Internal auditing (47.1%) generally had objectives set for only one year.

    C. Capital structure (63.2%), tax compliance (56.3%), asset management (85.6%), and financing cash requirements (55.6%) generally had objectives set for five years.

5. Examining measurable objectives:

    A. The current ratio (current assets to current liabilities) was most frequently mentioned (66.7% definitely).

      B.   Net profit after tax on net worth and average collection period were second and third percentages.

      C.   Net sales per dollar of depreciated fixed assets was least frequently mentioned (11.8% definitely).

      D.   Net sales per dollars of net working capital and cost sales per dollar of inventory were second and third from last percentages.

6.   Liquidity was the most frequently mentioned objective (current ratio), with profitability second (NPAT/NW and NPAT/net sales) and activity third (average collection period).

7.   The firms surveyed rated the effectiveness of their management team and their organization's communications very high. Planning in the organization and the performance appraisal system appear to need improvement.

Quotes/Observations from Interviews of Finance Executives

1.   Accountant/finance person is often not involved in the master plan-after the fact, or mostly used as a catch-up. He is generally brought in to confirm someone else's thoughts rather than at the beginning.

2.   The financial person has a better chance of respect if he has worked himself up from the bottom. How the CEO views the financial person has a great influence upon whether or not he/she is considered as being a major contributor to the strategic planning process.

3.   Financial persons are not involved in the strategic planning of most organizations.

4.   The financial person is viewed as the weakest link in the planning process.

5.   The financial plan is one leg of a three-legged plan, it should be part of the strategic plan. There is no strategic plan that overrides the financial plan.

6.   The financial plan is more a facilitator of the strategic plan.

7.   Financial people are making a more significant contribution to the strategic plan, because now CEOs are less dictatorial and more people are becoming involved.

8.   Some objectives will conflict, for example, in the case of cash flow and profitability. The decision will rest upon whether the firm is after cash flow

at a particular time or profitability. Strategies drive numbers; numbers don't drive strategies. Measurable objectives should be benchmarked:

A. Net profit after taxes on net worth

B. Net profit after taxes on net sales

C. Cost of sales per dollar of inventory

D. Current assets to current liabilities

E. Current and long-term liabilities to net worth

F. Break-even point (percent of capacity)

G. Average collection period

9. ROI would rather use invested capital, equity, and long-term debt as investment base.

10. Our company uses net profit after taxes on net worth, net profit after taxes on net sales, and current and long-term liabilities to net worth.

Conclusion

The senior executive of the finance function should play a major role in the development of the organization's strategic plan. In this role he wears first the hat of a team manager, but uses his functional expertise to interpret financial implications into the strategic plan. The strategic planning group, which incorporates major functional areas, works as a team to define purpose, analyzes the operating environment, assesses the organization's strengths and weaknesses, makes assumptions, and determines long-range objectives (Migliore, 1984, 1987). After the organization's total plan is developed, each functional manager must develop a support plan to assist the organization in achieving its purpose and stated long-term objectives.

Pro forma balance sheet and income statements should be developed by the finance function to support the expected results of the strategic plan. Cash should be managed strategically over the long term to enhance profitability and allocate scarce resources.

The survey indicated that the finance function was present in those companies that had three- to five-year long-range strategic planning. However, no conclusion could be reached as to the extent of their participation in integrating the financial implications with the long-term strategic plan.

Every organization should determine for itself the three to five key longterm financial objectives. These objectives should be reflected in the firm's overall strategic plan. Some measures of either return on capital or return on equity must be included. They join the firm's other overall objectives which might include total revenue, market share, productivity, human resources, and ethics.

The financial plan then should monitor all other financial benchmarks and ratios. If any of these indicators or ratios exceed a predefined range, they should be "red flagged" and reported to management. The overall strategic plan and financial plan should address the issues of which assets and divisions within the firm should need funds invested, what is the best source of funds, and what is the best mix of funds. Also to be considered is the dividend or capital appreciation strategy to the investors/owners of the firm.

Recommendations for expanding and improving the study would include expanding the study to a nationwide base with a much larger and diversified number of responses. The expanded study could include questions to probe the extent of the finance function participation in integrating the financial implications with the long-term strategic plan. Also, the analysis of smaller versus larger firms could be expanded to examine firms in each of the sales/revenue categories. Different industries could be examined separately as well as possibly public versus private firms and profit versus nonprofit firms. Also, the number of finance functions and measurable objectives could be expanded. Examples of financial objectives from actual plans:

1.   Bring accounts payable from 35 days in 1988 to 31days in 1989.

2.   Increase ROA from 5.3 percent to 6 percent by the end of 1989.

3.   Increase profit margin from 0.5 percent to 1 percent by end of 1989.

4.   Increase current ratio from 1.31X to 2 X by the end of fiscal year 1993.

5.   Increase debt/asset ratio from .73 to .55 by the end of fiscal year 1993.

6.   Keep times interest earned ratio at no lower than 10 X.

7.   Increase corporate PM to 3 percent by the end of fiscal year 1993.

8.   Increase return on assets to 10 percent by the end of fiscal year 1993.

9.   Increase return on equity to 25 percent by the end of fiscal year 1993.

10.   Increase PS/DD GM to 25 percent by the end of fiscal year 1993.

As a reminder, objectives can be set in the following areas:

Financial Return on Investment

1.   Net profit after taxes/net worth

2.   Net profit after taxes/total assets

3.   Net profit after taxes + depreciation + noncash expense/total assets

Return on Sales
1. Net sales per dollar of net worth
2. Net sales per dollar of total assets
3. Net sales per dollar of net working capital
4. Net profit after taxes/net sales
5. Cost of sales per dollar of inventory
6. New sales per dollar of depreciated fixed assets.

Financial Leverage
1. Debt/equity ratio
2. Total debt/total assets
3. Times interest earned.

Current Ratio
1. Current assets to current liabilities
2. Cash and receivables to current liabilities
3. Cash and equivalent to current liabilities
4. Current liabilities to net worth
5. Acid-test ratio (current assets-inventory)/(current liabilities).

Activity
1. Inventory turnover
2. Accounts receivable turnover
3. Average collection period
4. Total asset turnover
5. Fixed asset turnover.

Market Ratios
1. Earnings per share
2. Dividend per share
3. Dividend payout ratio
4. Book value per share
5. Price/earnings ratio
6. Dividend yield.

Appendix A

A study of the strategic planning practices of 62 major companies was conducted. A preliminary study of 38 (Study I) was conducted with a structured questionnaire and then expanded to 24 more (Study II) organizations. The results were discussed and more ideas gathered from ten financial officers of major organizations. The purpose was to determine specifically how both long- and short-range financial planning was being conducted. Companies with defined long-range plans have more financial input than those that focused on short-term planning. There is a different concept of financial planning in larger and smaller firms.

Information on financial tools used and other comparisons was presented. The authors concluded that a long-term financial plan must be developed to support a firm's overall strategic plan and that the chief financial officer should play a vital role in developing the firm's strategic plan. Finally, each firm should pick a minimum of three to five key long-term financial targets. All other financial ratios should be monitored and be part of the formal financial plan.

Appendix B
Results of Study I
Firms in Northeastern Oklahoma

The respondents had these definitions in responding to the questionnaire:

A. Strategic Planning is the philosophy of managing with a planning process. It is both a product and a process. The product is the plan itself. It is in writing and clearly defines where the organization intends to be in the long term, usually three to five years. The plan includes objectives, strategy, and the short-term steps to ensure overall success. The *process* is the interaction that takes place in developing the plan. Everyone involved in executing the plan should be involved in its development.

B. Functional Plans are developed to support the overall organizational strategic plan. Functional plans include the following areas: finance, manufacturing, personnel, research, marketing, etc. They use the same philosophy and process in the strategic planning definition.

C. Systems Approach is a view of the organization as a whole with interacting subsets. The financial plan is an element of the whole organizational plan. Systems thinking considers the action of each element and that each action or reaction affects other organizational functions. The systems approach considers that a firm operates as a dynamic organism with all parts, or subsystems, operating toward the common purpose of the firm as stated in its strategic plan. The firm's financial system provides the implementation of its strategic plan and is a segment of the total system.

D. Objective is a specific measurable result that outlines exactly what is to be accomplished within a time frame.

E. Strategy involves how, where, and when to commit resources to achieve objectives.

Study I Questions and Responses

1. Does the organization you work for (or local division) have regular strategic planning meetings that focus on three to five years?

    Yes: 81.6%   No: 18.4%   Don't Know: 0.0%
    a.   If the answer to question 1 is yes, how frequent are the planning meetings?

Weekly	0.0%	Semi-Annually	28.6%
Monthly	3.6%	Annually	50.0%
Quarterly	10.7%	Other (explain)	7.1%
		Don't Know	0.0%

    b.   What are titles of others in the meeting?

2.   Is someone from the finance function usually at these long-range strategic planning meetings?

        Yes: 96.9%   No: 3.1%   Don't Know: 0.0%

    a.   If the answer to question 2 was No, or Don't Know, go on to question 3.

    b.   If the answer to question 2 is Yes, how active is the finance participant on a scale of 1 to 5, with 1 being inactive and 5 being very active?

inactive	1	2	3	4	5	very active
	0.0%	9.7%	16.1%	19.4%		54.8%

3.   Are measurable overall organization objectives outlined in a few key areas for years 3 through 5? (Example revenue, sales, ROI, production, etc.)

        Yes: 78.4%   No: 21.6%   Don't Know: 0.0% 3A.

    a.   Are strategies developed to meet these objectives?
        Yes: 87.1%   No: 12.9%

4.   Does the finance function have measurable objectives for:

One year	Yes 94.1%	No 2.9%	Don't Know 2.9%
Three years	Yes 71.0%	No 22.6%	Don't Know 6.5%
Five years	Yes 48.4%	No 45.2%	Don't Know 6.5%

    a.   Does the finance function have specific strategies to meet the finance objectives?
        Yes: 85.7%   No: 5.7%   Don't Know: 8.6%

5.   If the answer to any part of question 4 is Yes, are measurable objectives set for the following functions within the finance discipline?

Yes

	One Year	Three Years	Five Years	No
Capital structure	42.1%	39.5%	1.6%	5.3%
Tax compliance	42.1%	18.4%	7.9%	26.3%
Tax planning	52.6%	28.9%	18.4%	21.1%
Accounting policies	47.4%	10.5%	13.2%	15.8%
Financial reporting	52.6%	15.8%	15.8%	15.8%

Financing cash	68.4%	44.7%	26.3%	2.6%
Requirements cash management	63.2%	26.3%	21.1%	5.3%
Pension plan investment	18.4%	13.2%	7.9%	50.0%
Performance internal auditing	28.9%	0.0%	7.9%	36.8%
Foreign exchange	23.7%	7.9%	5.3%	52.6%
Exposure risk management	42.1%	21.1%	13.2%	34.2%
Payout ratios	23.7%	5.3%	15.8%	34.2%
Asset management	55.3%	31.6%	23.7%	13.2%

6. Are   measurable   objectives   set   for   the   following?

	Yes	No
Net profit after taxes on net worth	77.1%	22.9%
Net profit after taxes on net sales	58.8%	41.2%
Net sales per dollar of net worth	16.7%	83.3%
Net sales per dollar of total assets	31.3%	68.7%
Net sales per dollar of net working capital	40.0%	60.0%
Cost of sales per dollar of inventory	46.7%	53.3%
Net sales per dollar of depreciated fixed assets	6.7%	93.3%
Current assets to current liabilities	73.5%	26.5%
Cash and receivables to current liabilities	36.7%	63.3%
Cash and equivalent to current liabilities	33.3%	66.7%
Funded debt to net working capital	30.3%	69.7%
Inventories to net working capital	13.3%	86.7%
Net fixed assets to net worth	22.6%	77.4%
Current liabilities to net worth	25.8%	74.2%
Current and long-term liabilities to net worth	66.7%	33.3%
Accumulated depreciation to original cost of fixed assets	19.4%	80.6%
Break-even point (% of capacity)	33.3%	66.7%
Average collection period	60.0%	40.0%

Breakdown Of Comparison In Study I

	Million
5.6%	$5 or less
0.0	6 to 10
13.9	10 to 50
13.9	51to 100
66.7	over $100
0.0	Don't Know

Appendix C
Results of Study II
Firms in State of Oklahoma

1.   Does your organization set objectives that are specific and quantifiable, and outline exactly what is to be accomplished in the future?

   (86.4%) 1 Yes   (13.6%) 2 No

   a.   Are these objectives written down?
   (86.4%) 1 Yes   (9.1%) 2 No   (4.5%) 3 Don't Know.

   b.   How long are these written objectives for? (Check all which apply.)
   5 years (45.5% said yes)

   2-4 years (45.5% said yes)   1 year (63.6% said yes)

2.   Does the organization (or local division) you work for have regular strategic planning meetings that focus on three to five years?

   (63.6%) 1 Yes   (31.8%)2 No   (4.5%) 3 Don't Know

   a.   If the answer to question 2 is yes, how frequent are the planning meetings? (Check the most appropriate one.)
   (0.0%) 1 Weekly   (33.3%) 4 Semiannually
   (6.7%) 2 Monthly   (26.7%) 5 Annually
   (20.0%) 3 Quarterly   (13.3%) 6 Other (explain)

   b.   What are the titles of others in the meeting?

   c.   How many are involved in the planning meetings?
   Mean = 10.1 persons   Median = 10 persons

3.   Does the organization you work for have a separate strategic planning department?

   (22.7%) 1 Yes   (72.7%)2 No   (4.5%) 3 Don't Know

   a.   If the answer to question 3 is yes, how frequent are their meetings? (Check the most appropriate one.)
   (40.0%) 1 Weekly   (0.0%) 4 Semiannually
   (20.0%) 2 Monthly   (0.0%) 5 Annually
   (20.0%) 3 Quarterly   (0.0%) 6 Other (explain)
   (20.0%) 7 Don't Know

4. Do each of your major divisions or functional areas in your company have regular planning meetings that focus on 3 to 5 years?

    (45.5%) 1 Yes   (45.5%)2 No   (9.1%) 3 Don't Know

5. Is someone from the finance function usually at these long range strategic meetings?

    (88.2%) 1 Yes   (11.8%) 2 No   (0.0%) 3 Don't Know

If the answer to question was No or Don't Know, go on to question 6.

a. If the answer to question is Yes, how active is the finance participant- on a scale of 1 to 5, with 1 being inactive and 5 being very active? (Circle the most appropriate number.)

inactive	1	2	3	4	5	very active
	0.0%	0.0%	26.7%	53.3%	20.0%	

6. For how long does the finance function have measurable objectives?

One year		
Yes: (85.7%)	No: (9.5%)	Don't Know: (4.8%)3
Three years		
Yes: (50.0%)	No: (35.0%)	Don't Know: (15.0%)
Five years		
Yes: (45.5%)	No: (36.4%)	Don't Know: (18.2%)

a. Does the finance function have specific strategies to meet the finance objectives?

    (86.4%) 1 Yes   (9.1%) 2 No   (4.5%) 3 Don't Know

If the answer to any part of question 6 is Yes, are measurable objectives set for the following function within the finance discipline?

Maximum Length of Time Mentioned	One Year	Yes Three Years	Five Years	No
Capital structure	21.1%	15.8%	63.2%	0.0%
Tax compliance	25.0%	6.3%	56.3%	12.5%
Tax planning	26.7%	13.3%	46.7%	13.3%
Accounting policies	27.8%	16.7%	50.0%	5.6%
Financial reporting	27.8%	16.7%	50.0%	5.6%
Financing cash requirements	22.2%	22.2%	55.6%	0.0%
Cash management	42.1%	21.1%	36.8%	0.0%
Pension plan investment performance	17.6%	11.8%	41.2%	29.4%
Internal auditing	47.1%	5.9%	35.3%	11.8%
Foreign exchange exposure	7.1%	7.1%	14.3%	71.4%
Risk management	20.0%	6.7%	46.7%	26.7%
Payout ratios	15.4%	7.7%	38.5%	38.5%
Asset management	27.8%	11.1%	55.6%	5.6%

7. Are measurable objectives set for the following? (Circle the most appropriate number.)

	Avg. Score	Defi-nitely 1	Most of the Time 2	Some-times 3	Seldom 4	Never 5	Rank
A. Net profit after taxes on net worth	2.24	(52.9%)	(11.8%)	(11.8%)	(5.9%)	(17.6%)	2
B. Net profit after taxes on net sales	2.39	(50.0%)	(11.1%)	(11.1%)	(5.6%)	(22.2%)	4
C. Net sales per dollar of net worth	3.53	(17.6%)	(5.9%f	(23.5%)	(11.8%)	(41.2%)	15
D. Net sales per dollar of total assets	3.22	(27.8%)	(0.0%)	(27.8%)	(11.1%)	(33.3%)	UT
E. Net sales per dollar of net working capital	3.71	(17.6%)	(0.0%)	(17.6%)	(23.5%)	(41.2%)	17
F. Cost of sales per dollar of inventory	3.61	(27.8%)	(0.0%)	(5.6%)	(16.7%)	(50.0%)	16
G. Net sales per dollar of depreciated fixed assets	4.06	(11.8%)	(5.9%)	(11.8%)	(5.9%)	(64.7%)	18
H. Current assets to current liabilities	2.00	(66.7%)	(0.0%)	(16.7%)	(0.0%)	(16.7%)	1
I. Cash and receivables to current liabilities	2.44	(55.6%)	(0.0%)	(16.7%)	(0.0%)	(27.8%)	5
J. Cash and equivalent to current liabilities	2.88	(41.2%)	(0.0%)	(23.5%)	(0.0%)	(35.3%)	9

		1	2	3	4	5	
K. Funded debt to net working capital	2.76	(41.2%)	(11.8%)	(5.9%)	(11.8%)	(29.4%)	8
L. Inventories to net working capital	3.50	(27.8%)	(0.0%)	(11.1%)	(16.7%)	(44.4%)	14
M. Net fixed assets to net worth	3.17	(33.3%)	(0.0%)	(22.2%)	(5.6%)	(38.9%)	10
N. Current liabilities to net worth	2.59	(52.9%)	(5.9%)	(5.9%)	(0.0%)	(35.3%)	6T
O. Current and long-term liabilities to net worth	2.59	(41.2%)	(17.6%)	(11.8%)	(0.0%)	(29.4%)	6T
P. Accumulated depreciation to original cost of fixed assets	3.24	(23.5%)	(17.6%)	(11.8%)	(5.9%)	(41.2%)	B
Q. Break-even point (% of capacity)	3.22	(27.8%)	(16.7%)	(5.6%)	(5.6%)	(44.4%)	11T
R. Average collection period	2.26	(52.6%)	(15.8%)	(5.3%)	(5.3%)	(21.1%)	3

Circle the number that most closely describes your feelings on questions 8-14.

8.   An organization should use the type of management described in the definition for strategic planning.

(9.1%)	(4.5%)	(9.1%)	(36.4%)	(40.9%)
1	2	3	4	5
DISAGREE		NOT SURE		AGREE
Average Score = 3.95				

9.   I would rate the effectiveness of our entire management team as:

(0.0%)	(0.0%)	(13.6%)	(54.5%)	(31.8%)
1	2	3	4	5
POOR		AVERAGE		EXCELLENT
Average Score = 4.18				

10.   I would rate the communication in our organization as:

(0.0%)	(0.0%)	(27..3%)	(50.0%)	(22.7%)
1	2	3	4	5
POOR		AVERAGE		EXCELLENT
Average Score = 3.95				

11. I would rate the planning in our organization as:

(0.0%)	(0.0%)	(31.8%)	(50.0%)	(9.1%)
1	2	3	4	5
POOR		AVERAGE		EXCELLENT
Average Score = 3.59				

12. I would rate the performance appraisal system in this organization as:

(0.0%)	(4.5%)	(45.5%)	(40.9%)	(9.1%)
1	2	3	4	5
POOR		AVERAGE		EXCELLENT
Average Score = 3.59				

13. Do you feel that financial planning is applicable and beneficial for your firm and the industry you are in?

(0.0%)	(4.5%)	(4.5%)	(18.2%)	(72.7%)
1	2	3	4	5
DISAGREE		NOT SURE		AGREE
Average Score = 4.59				

14. Sales/revenue of your company or local division.

(1)	$5 or less	(4.5%)	(4)	51 to 100	(13.6%)
(2)	6 to 10	(0.0%)	(5)	Over $100	(68.2%)
(3)	10 to 50	(4.5%)	(6)	Don't Know	(9.1%)

References

Allen, M. G. "Strategic Management Hits Its Stride". *Planning Review*. Sept 13(5), 1985: 6-45.

Allio, R. J. and Pennington, W.M. *Corporate Planning: Techniques and Applications*, New York: AMACOM, 1979.

Bergson, L. "The CFO as Corporate Strategist." *Institutional*, 1980.

Carleton, W. T. and Davis, J. V. "Financing of Strategic Action." From *Strategic Planning to Strategic Management*, Ed. Ansoff, H. I. Chichester, England: John Wiley, 1976.

Donaldson, G. "Financial Goals and Strategic Consequences." *Harvard Business Review*. May/June 1985: 37-36.

Donnelly, R. M. "Controller's Role in Corporate Planning." *Managerial Planning* (3), 1981.

Duhaine, I. M. and Thomas, H. "Financial Analysis and Strategic Management." *Journal of Economics and Business* 35(3-4), 1983: 413-440.

Grawoig and Hubbard. *Strategic Financial Planning with Simulation*. New York: Petrocelli Books, 1982.

Higgins, R. C. "How Much Growth Can a Firm Afford?" *Financial Management*. Fall, 1977: 7.

Krackou, L. M. and Kaushik, S. K. *The Practical Financial Manager*. New York: New York Institute of Finance, 1988.

Lamberson, M. "A Survey of Financial Structure Management Practices of Manufacturers: A Comparison of Large and Small Firms." 27 Jan. 1988.

Malermee, J. K. and Jaffe, G. "An Integrative Approach to Strategic and Financial Planning". *Managerial Planning*, Jan./Feb.1985.

Migliore, R. H. *An MBO Approach to Long-Range Planning*. Englewood Cliffs: Prentice Hall. 1984.

Migliore, R. H. *Strategic Long-Range Planning*. Tulsa: Western Publishing, 1987.

Migliore, R. H. and Haines, S. *Human Resource Planning-a Competitive Advantage; A Redefinition of the Field*. Submitted to Academy of Management Review. August. 1988.

Migliore, R. H. and Stevens, R. E., *"A Marketing View of MBO Managerial Planning."* March/April 1980.

Migliore, R. H. and Thrun, W. *Developing a Strategic Plan for Production*. Tulsa: J. Williams Publishing. 1988.

Robinson, R. B., Jr. and Pearce, J. A., II. "The Impact of Formalized Strategic Planning on Financial Performance in Small Organizations," *Strategic Management*, 4(3), 1983: 197-207.

Stanch, P. J. and Zaragoza, C. E., "Strategic Funds Programming: The Missing Link in Corporate Planning." *Managerial Planning*, 4(3), 1980: 3.

Vander Weele, R., "Expanded Role of Controllership in Strategic Planning." *Managerial Planning*, 29(2), 1980: 16.

Wall Street Journal, "Long-Range Plans," 31 Oct. 1986.

CHAPTER 8
CAPITAL BUDGETING
How It Fits into the Firm's Financial Plan and Supports the Overall Strategic Plan

After years of experience consulting and working with organizations of all sizes and in a wide variety of industries, I have observed that in many organizations there is lack of coordination between the capital budget, financial plan, and the organization's overall strategic plan.

Several years ago, the topic of capital budgeting and how it supported the overall plan was raised at a corporate budget meeting. The reaction was that no one seemed to be able to pinpoint the answer. Continued inquiry into corporate practices indicated that there was, in many cases, little connection between the capital budget, financial plan, and the firm's overall strategic plan.

Review of Literature

The following articles suggest relationships among strategic planning, financial planning, and capital budgeting. Each gives a different perspective of the relationship.

The article, "Financial Goals and Strategic Consequences" demonstrates how a company can check whether its strategic and financial goals are consistent with reality. Such an analysis may better prepare the company to make the right trade-offs among conflicting goals and to anticipate what the consequences of its actions may be (Donaldson, 1985). Donaldson lists certain characteristics of corporate financial goals systems that have often been overlooked and that contribute to misunderstanding of the goal-setting process. Contrary to popular belief, companies do not put maximum profit before all else.

> Mature companies assign priorities to multiple financial goals based on the relative power of the economic constituencies represented by these individual goals.

> Companies do not have an inalienable right to "dream the impossible dream" and set any goal.

> Managing a company's financial goals system is an unending process in which competing and conflicting priorities must be balanced.

A company's internal capital market must continuously try to reconcile the demand for and supply of funds.

Most managers find it difficult to understand and accept the entire goal system. Although financial goals appear objective and precise, they are in fact relative, changeable, and unstable. Moreover, subordinate managers normally see them from the limited perspective of their immediate responsibilities (Donaldson, 1985:58). By recognizing that all financial goals are interdependent, a company soon learns that a change in one demands a compensating adjustment somewhere else in the funds-flow equation (Donaldson, 1985).

In the article, "Financial Planning System and MBO-An Integrated Approach" Garg states a financial planning system (FPS) integrated with MBO can offer great potential for management. Furthermore, he says that an integrated FPS with MBO is a managerial process which does not sacrifice the financial good of the firm but rather instills in the employee a sense of commitment and desire to contribute to commitment and desire to contribute to organizational financial goals (Garg, R. C., 1983). Garg affirms:

The relationships between finance and management are intimate ones in principle. Management must have a comprehensive financial plan in order to accomplish organizational goals. At the same time, no financial plan can be effective unless it is integrated with the managerial planning system. Combining these two systems of managerial practice can help generate synergistic effects in the functioning of an organization. Both FPS and MBO are to be viewed as mutually reinforcing (Garg,1983).

An integrated version of the FPS with MBO will help in setting financial goals which are mutually acceptable and feasible to the top management and subordinates. Both the conceptualization and the implementation of the financial plan will have the approval of top as well as middle management, as long as the participative management practices are followed (Garg, 1983).

Stonich and Zaragoza's article, "Strategic Funds Programming: The Missing Link in Corporate Planning" deals with an approach, strategic funds programming (SFP), that helps companies make strategy happen. SFP is a management system designed to help organizations isolate potential programs having an impact on the future of the business and then to make decisions about which programs to undertake. Thus, concrete actions are taken that affect the future performance of the organization (Stonich and Zaragoza, 1980).

Malernee and Jaffe, in "An Integrative Approach to Strategic and Financial Planning," state that the financial implications of either strategy formulation or implementation are often given only a cursory glance or completely ignored, but that recent environmental changes have forced many CEOs to question the viability, and even feasibility, of their originally developed strategic plans. This article offers an integrative approach to strategic and financial planning (Malernee and Jaffe, 1980).

In this article, "A Program For Integrating Budgeting and MBO" Babcock and Qureshi develop a methodology for operationalizing the integration of budgeting and MBO. They claim that both budgeting and MBO can be strengthened and mutually supportive by creating a unified MBO-budgeting system, rather than treating MBO and budgeting as separate processes. The result is the development and funding of operational objectives and budgets that effectively allow the enterprise to carry on its ongoing activities, as well as encourage continuing attention to supplemental activities (Babcock and Qureshi, 1980).

Dickinson and Herbst, in "Understand Deficiencies of Capital Budgeting Techniques Before Applying Them to Planning" attribute much of the controversy of applying capital budgeting methods to marketing decisions to the fact that the executives who use the methods do so without understanding the implied assumptions. These authors state that the mathematical theorists who developed the capital budgeting methods' assumptions are not based on realistic assumptions such as:

> Perfect capital markets exist (that is, the markets appropriately reflect all relevant factors pertaining to the company and all firms have equal access to the capital markets).

> Net, after-tax cash flows are appropriately reflected over the total life of the investment alternative, to infinity.

> The singular goal is to maximize the current value of cash flow (Dickinson and Herbst, 1984).

The article discusses the payback period and the discounted cash flow methods: net present value and the internal rate of return. The payback period method is the time it takes to recover the initial investment. Or, stated another way, it is the return *of* investment. The discounted cash flow methods, internal rate of return, and net present value take into account the time value of money and are directed toward the return *on* investment. From the standpoint of marketers, for the discounted cash flow to be utilized effectively in making decisions before the planning takes place, six guidelines to use are:

1. Develop understanding. Being aware of the assumption of the DCF techniques will certainly give a healthy skepticism.

2. Establish different hurdles rates. Qualitatively attractive long-term alternatives should be subjected to lower rates of discount.

3. Set a low discount rate. Insist on justification of requests in terms of their impact on strategy.

4. Use a sequential procedure. Qualitative factors such as mission or image should be constraints on alternative investments.

5. Mix methods. There is no one best method of quantitatively evaluating investment alternatives. Payback, average return on average investment, net present value, internal rate of return, and computer simulation all can provide useful insights.

6. Seek new methods. Marketers and others faced with uncertainty will have to develop new methods to suit their specific needs (Dickinson and Herbst, 1984).

In "The Relationship Between Long-Term Strategy and Capital Budgeting" Steven D. Grossman and Richard Lindhe maintain that capital investment decisions on the program level and specific asset level should be made in conjunction with the objectives, of the organization as a whole. To meet these objectives capital budgeting should be reflected in the short- and long-term strategies. The organization's long-term plan is less imprecise than the short-term plan. However, the organization must understand and monitor the environment in which it will exist and define its resources. Once the organization has done this, it can establish strategies for the short- and long-term plan to meet its objectives.

The authors point out two problems that exist with the present value model in the capital budgeting process. First, the measurement of elements by use of the present value model does not accurately depict the most desirable alternative in a set of alternatives. They agree with Dickinson and Herbst that a mix of measurement devices is needed. Second, the present value model does not justify how a capital investment decision will interrelate with other elements or parts of the organization. They further argue, "the value of an organization is greater than the sum of its parts, because the special combination of resources and their use derives greater return than the sum of the return of each of those resources used independently" (Grossman and Lindhe, 1984).

Connection with Overall Plan

The strategic plan is a flexible, dynamic, and continuous plan that assumes a democratic or participative style of management. It integrates various plans by providing appropriate linkage between short- and long-term plans. Its purpose is to allocate scarce resources in order to ensure continuous achievement of long-term objectives (Vander Weele, 1980). The strategic plan's objectives should be specific, measurable, and in a time frame. However, there are objectives that are not directly related to the strategic long-range plan. For example, customer service could lead to increased market share but not be directly aimed at return on investment. The prologue to all functional plans is strategy. The driving force of all strategic planning is the implementation of strategies. After the strategic plan is developed, marketing, production, human resources, finance, and other support plans are developed. Mark Kirk, corporate controller of Purolator Products Company, said, "Strategies drive numbers; numbers don't drive strategies. Good strategies don't produce bad numbers, the unknown element is *time*."

Note Figure 8-1 which shows the relationship between these plans.

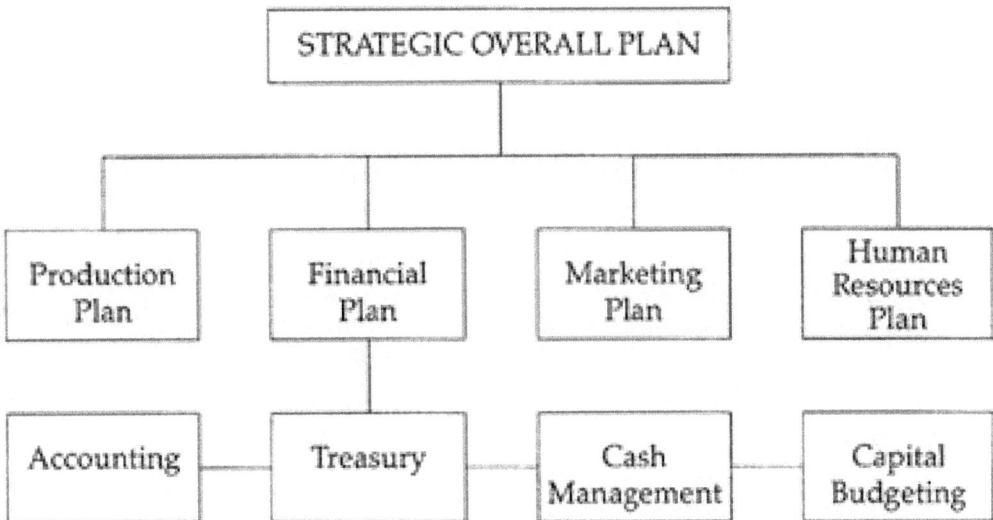

```
                    ┌─────────────────────────────┐
                    │   STRATEGIC OVERALL PLAN     │
                    └─────────────────────────────┘
                                  │
   ┌──────────────┬───────────────┼───────────────┬──────────────┐
┌──────────┐  ┌──────────┐   ┌──────────┐   ┌──────────────┐
│Production│  │Financial │   │Marketing │   │   Human      │
│   Plan   │  │   Plan   │   │   Plan   │   │ Resources    │
└──────────┘  └──────────┘   └──────────┘   │   Plan       │
                    │                        └──────────────┘
┌──────────┐  ┌──────────┐   ┌──────────┐   ┌──────────────┐
│Accounting│──│ Treasury │───│   Cash   │───│   Capital    │
└──────────┘  └──────────┘   │Management│   │  Budgeting   │
                             └──────────┘   └──────────────┘
```

The Financial Plan and Capital Budgeting

The financial plan supports the strategic plan. It is that integral part of the strategic plan that permeates all other functional plans of an organization. The financial plan has its own purpose, environmental analysis, strengths and weaknesses, assumptions, objectives, strategy, operational plans, and controls. The plan contains projections of income statement, balance sheet, budgets, cash flow, and sources and uses of funds. It is a forecast of future monetary needs of an organization and the development of ways to generate cash flows to meet the objectives of the strategic plan. Its predictions and forecast illustrate what an organization has to sell or produce to *ultimately* maximize owners' wealth. The theory that a company's main purpose is to maximize shareholders' or owners' wealth is not always the most important issue. Financial objectives and strategic objectives are sometimes at opposing ends. Finance may have a need to decrease production costs while the strategic objective is to increase sales. Companies must assign priorities with conflicting and competing objectives. The monitoring of financial objectives is a continuous ongoing process. The financial performance of an organization depends upon how well the financial plan supports the strategic plan.

The classical concept of capital budgeting decisions is for the firm to accept investment proposals up to that point where marginal costs equal revenues. Firms are restrained from accepting all capital investment proposals. Projects are ranked and based upon some mathematical standard and undertaken until the point reached where either funds are not available or the project's return falls below the firm's hurdle rate (Sherman, 1978). Some projects are accepted qualitatively, such as those that are mandatory and/or nonfinancial proposals such as pollution devices, safety programs, or employee benefits. Some proposals are accepted so a company may remain competitive to maintain customer relations, or even to defend its market share.

> Capital budgeting is an integral part of overall corporate objectives, since the objectives provide a framework within which capital budgets must develop. A capital budget is a plan to achieve corporate objectives. Capital budgets may embrace such projects as increasing plant capacity, modernizing equipment, gaining control of a supplier or competitor, expanding a product line, or implementing other cost-saving programs. Capital budgeting concerns include allocating funds among alternate investment proposals so as to optimize long-term profits to the shareholders (Vaughn, Norgarn, and Bennett, 1972).

Only strategically defined, thoroughly thought-out qualitative and quantitative capital budgeting proposals will achieve the future expectations of the organization.

Capital budgeting is a subset of the financial plan. It is the process of allocating resources among ideas, projects, and products and then quantitatively and/or qualitatively evaluating alternatives to determine the best investment to be used in the financial plan. It has a synergistic effect; that is, the total effect is greater than the sum of two effects taken independently. It is the most dynamic aspect of the decision-making process. The dynamics of capital budgeting involve many variables. However, the variables are not isolated from each other. They must interact together with an optimal decision (Truitt, 1985).

Capital budgeting is at the very heart of virtually all financial planning. In many instances this perspective is not fully appreciated because the term "capital budgeting" has become too associated with the mechanics of DCF economics and yearly, short-term budgeting. In fact, however, key decisions of any planning process, short-term operational, or long-term strategy is the determination of which "project" will be funded and pursued to meet the corporation's goals. This is a capital budgeting decision; it is a basic part of planning (Hoyle, 1978).

Principal Mathematical Techniques Used in Capital Budgeting

Payback Period is the length of time to pay back the original investment. Advantage: simplicity. Disadvantages: does not recognize the time value of money or revenues generated beyond the payback period. *Discounted Cash Flow Rate of Return* (internal rate of return) equates present value of the future cash flows with the present value of the original cash outlay. Advantages: Recognizes time value of money, provides for project ranking with the assumption of cost of capital, emphasizes long-term profitability, and recognizes cash flows beyond the payback period. Disadvantages: trial-and-error procedure and difficult to understand.

Return on Investment (accounting rate of return) measures operations' performance by dividing the average annual income by the assets committed. It is used in planning and evaluation of operations because these functions are enhanced by the ability to examine the components separately. Advantages: Identifies ways to increase returns, is easily understood and offers a basis of comparison against results from existing investments and operations. Disadvantages: Does not recognize time value of money and the real difficulty of ascertaining a "true" income figure and an acceptable measurement of the assets committed. Net Present Value determines the dollar difference between the present value of the investment outlay and the present value of the yearly cash flows measured against the firm's hurdle rate is the minimum acceptable rate of return. A positive net amount means the project meets the minimum requirements. Advantages: recognizes time value of money.

Disadvantages: Hurdle rate is difficult to determine and cash flows are assumed to be reinvested at a constant rate which may not be justifiable. *Benefit-Cost Ratio*(profitability index or present value index) is measured by dividing the present value of the cash flows by the present value of the original investment using the same hurdle rate as used in net present value. Advantages: Recognizes time value of money and establishes a "break-even point" of 1.0. Disadvantages: Requires additional calculations and no positive reference to time frame and cash flows (Sherman, 1978).

No matter how sophisticated the capital budgeting techniques are, they first must integrate four major analyses into the decision-making process (Sherman, 19778).

These four interdependent steps are: (1) the defining and the communication of a firm's long-range and strategic plans and goals, (2) the development of a system that permits the orderly gathering and ranking of investment proposal, (3) the determination of the accuracy of the estimates that become utilized in the estimated rate of return calculations, and (4) the determination and assignment of the probabilities of levels of risk to the investment proposals. It is only after due consideration of all these steps as an integrated whole has been taken that a valid "go or no go" decision can be made in regard to capital budgeting decision (Sherman, 1978).

Conclusion and Recommendation

Capital budgeting fits into the firm's financial plan and supports the overall strategic plan through its future economic benefits to an organization. Its prime decision-making factors are time value of money, cost of capital, and the inherent risk of each project/proposal. Our discussion targets fixed assets. Fixed assets are capable of being used repeatedly over a long period of time and used in the normal course of business. They are long-term present dollar commitments. The capital budgeting decisions to finance these commitments must be made strategically. These decisions are more than far-reaching, they are future reaching.

The consensus of opinion is that the ultimate goal of an organization is to maximize shareholders' or owners' wealth. Maximization is determined by a firm's use of assets, financing of assets, and planning and forecasting. The mechanics of capital budgeting: Payback, Discounted Cash Flow Rate of Return (Internal Rate of Return), Return on Investment, Benefit-Cost Ratio are all paramount to the success of a firm or company in its bid to maximize shareholder wealth.

Firms can identify their target markets in terms of geographical location, consumption habits, levels of income, and levels of education, and then create new products to maintain and increase market share. There is an underlying issue of who are a firm's customers not only today, but tomorrow? Capital budgeting decisions must address this issue today. As a starting point, one fact is established. The class of 2000 entered the first grade in 1988. How many are there? Who are they? More importantly, who are their parents? How many parents are customers of a particular industry? Parents influence children's purchasing decisions. Will the birth rate and life expectancy decrease or increase? How sophisticated will their level of education be? How consumer-oriented will they be? How will a firm's mission enhance their quality of life? Another factor that should influence capital budgeting decisions should be how a firm will favor in the coming external environment: short- and long-term interest rates, suppliers, local, state, national, and international governments and competitors, tax laws, and new legislation that will affect financial institutions.

The baby boomers are the largest consumer group in the United States. These people were born between 1946 and 1964. As this population gets progressively older, how will a firm's capital budgeting decisions affect them? How many are presently customers? What is their level of education? How consumer oriented are they? How politically active are they? What services will they demand? The class of 2000 and the baby boomers are two unique and distinct groups with their own inherent needs. These customers when asked the same questions about their needs will give unique and distinct and even opposing answers. Before the allocation of scarce resources become committed, management must take a hard and unbiased look at who are the customers, what they need now, and what they will need in the future. Consumers may need fewer nursing homes and more home health programs, fewer cars and more public transportation, fewer malls and more discount stores, fewer homes and more condominiums. These capital budgeting issues need to be addressed now, and not when the problems arise.

An organization's strategic planning must be receptive and take into account a changing society. The firm must have a willingness to communicate with economists, demographers, urban planners, social scientists, political scientists, health care experts, and others in order to monitor trends. Companies and institutions who investigate the above issues will be able to make a more profitable transition into the twenty-first century. Success in the year 2000 will depend on a well thought out strategic direction. The finance function supports this strategic plan. Capital budgeting decisions support the financial plan, and insure that capital is distributed to assets that are used as a base upon which the execution of the strategy is built.

References

Babcock, R. and Qureshi, M. A. *"A Proposal for Integrating Budgeting and MBO."* *Managerial Planning,* 29(6), 1981: 28..

Dickinson, R. A. and Herbst, A."Understand Deficiencies of Capital Budgeting Techniques Before Applying Them to Planning" *Marketing News,* March 16:10-11, 1984.

Donaldson,G."Financial Goals and Strategic Consequences" *Harvard Business Review,* May/June:1985:57-62.

Garg, R. C. "Financial Planning System and MBO: An Integrated Approach" *Managerial Planning,* XXXI(4) Jan./Feb.1983: 29-31. Grossman, S.D. and Lindhe, R."The Relationship Between Long-Term Strategy and Capital Budgeting"*Journal of Business Strategy* Fall:1984:105.

Grossman, S. D. and Lindhe, R. "The Relationship Between Long-Term Strategy and Capital Budgeting." *Journal of Business Strategy*, Fall, 1984: 105.

Hoyle, R. S. "Capital Budgeting Models and Planning: An Evolutionary Process" *Managerial Planning,* XXVII (3) 24 Nov./Dec.1978.

Malernee, J. K., Jr. and Jaffe, G."An Integrative Approach to Strategic and Financial Planning" *Managerial Planning.* XXX(4) Jan./Feb.1980:35.

Migliore, R. H. Hall, M. J. and Martin, R. T. "Financial Planning and the Organization's Strategic Plan" Paper submitted to the Academy of Management, 1988.

Schall, L. D. and Hatley, C. W. *Introduction to Financial Management.* New York:McGraw-Hill, 1986.

Sherman, J. F. "An Integration Approach to Capital Budgeting Decisions" *Managerial Planning,* XXVII (1) July/Aug. 1978:28-34.

Stonich, P. J. and Zaragoza, C. E."Strategic Funds Programming: The Missing Link to Corporate Planning." *Managerial Planning,.* XXIX (2) Sept./Oct. 1980:3.

Truitt, J. F. "Synergism: The Forgotten Capital Budgeting Dimension." *Managerial Planning,* XXXIII (5) March/April 1985:46.

Vander Weele, R. "The Expanded Role of Controllership in Strategic Planning." *Managerial Planning,* XXIX (2) Sept/Oct 1980:17.

Vaughn, D. E., Norgarro, R. L., and Bennett, H. *Financial Planning and Management: A Budgetary Approach.* New York: Goodyear Publishing Company, 1972.

CHAPTER 9
HUMAN RESOURCE PLANNING
A Competitive Business Advantage, A Redefinition of the Field

The Human Resource Planning (HRP) function can lead to a competitive business advantage if an organization chooses to put its emphasis in developing an aggressive, spirited, well-trained and motivated work force.

This chapter traces the evolution of HRP and suggests the next stage of evolution is a redefinition of the field. HRP can become specifically tailored and linked to the four hierarchical levels of a firm's strategic business planning, as adapted from the strategic literature.

Further, this chapter delineates a specific and clear strategic planning philosophy and process that an organization could use to define its strategic direction and tie the human resource plans to it.

Finally, research is discussed that shows firms who strategically plan and manage using their people power have a competitive business advantage.

It has been estimated that the amount of change in the world that occurred in the first 85 years of the 1900s will be matched within the last 15 years of this century. As a result, every company today is facing radical changes in their business. For example, approximately ten million U.S. workers lost their jobs between 1984 and 1988. In 1989, 116 million Americans had jobs. Those jobs are a result of rapid change. Companies with 1-19 employees accounted for 28 percent of the job expansion, and firms with over 5,000 employees lost 13.5 percent. This occurred through a myriad of circumstances including takeovers, mergers, plant closings, deregulation, downsizings, etc., according to the U.S. Department of Labor. These internal business changes may include the downsizings, mergers, global competition, competitive pressures. Technology and government may also include changes such as a turnaround, a culture change, a high growth situation, a total company transformation, new business start-ups, reorganizations, changing business strategies, cost cutting, repositioning and the like. The ability to successfully manage the complex change, stress, and human aspects associated with this have never been greater.

The need for proactive planning for a firm's attraction, motivation, growth, retention and/or contraction of its human resources has not kept pace with this amount of change in today's world. The proof can be seen in the large number of firms who go from expansion of their workforce to laying off thousands of workers soon afterwards. The planning for a firm's human resources in the broadest sense of those words can, instead, actually be a competitive business advantage.

The organizational area that is responsible for this planning is the Human Resource (HR) function. Within HR, the human resource planning field (HRP) has evolved into its present state over the last half of this century.

This article traces this evolution, and suggests that there needs to be a next level of HRP evolution in order for it to become fully effective, meaningful and relevant to the senior management of organizations. Only then does HR and HRP have the potential to become a bottom-line competitive business advantage for a firm.

This chapter will give an overview of the HRP field and its early developments. It will then explore the differing aspects of the field as it has evolved into a more mature professional discipline. The current state of the art will then be discussed along with some conclusions and a re-definition of the HRP field. Finally issues and barriers to the successful implementation of these new HRP concepts will be discussed. These barriers must be overcome if the promise of HRP as a competitive business advantage is to be fulfilled.

Overview of Human Resource Planning

The notion that a five-year strategic human resources plan is necessary seems to be a novel idea as we begin the last decade of the century. Paul F. Buller reports, "A few studies using more systematic empirical methods have recently appeared in the literature. These studies suggest that high levels of integration between human resources and strategic planning activities do not exist in most large firms" (Paul F. Buller). Stella M. Nkomo did a survey of Fortune 500 firms indicating that 54 percent prepare formal strategic human resources plans with only 15 percent using comprehensive systems. Few firms in the survey reported on integrated linkage between human resources planning and strategic business planning. Nkomo reports "What is clear from this survey is that formal strategic human resources planning is still in its infancy even among Fortune 500 firms. This result suggests that the literature is far ahead of actual organizational practices. The prevailing assumption of most line managers is that appropriate human resources can be found on short notice. Second, strategic planning for human resources has generally lagged behind planning for capital and financial resources. The human resources dimension of planning has been largely treated as a short-term implementation issue rather than a driving force in the formulation of strategic plans (Stella M. Nkomo).

Darrin Harwood, a recent Northeastern State University graduate, worked with me to determine how Muskogee, Oklahoma, area manufacturing firms were using human resources planning. We concluded approximately the same results as Nkomo.

Figure 9.1
Human Resource Planning

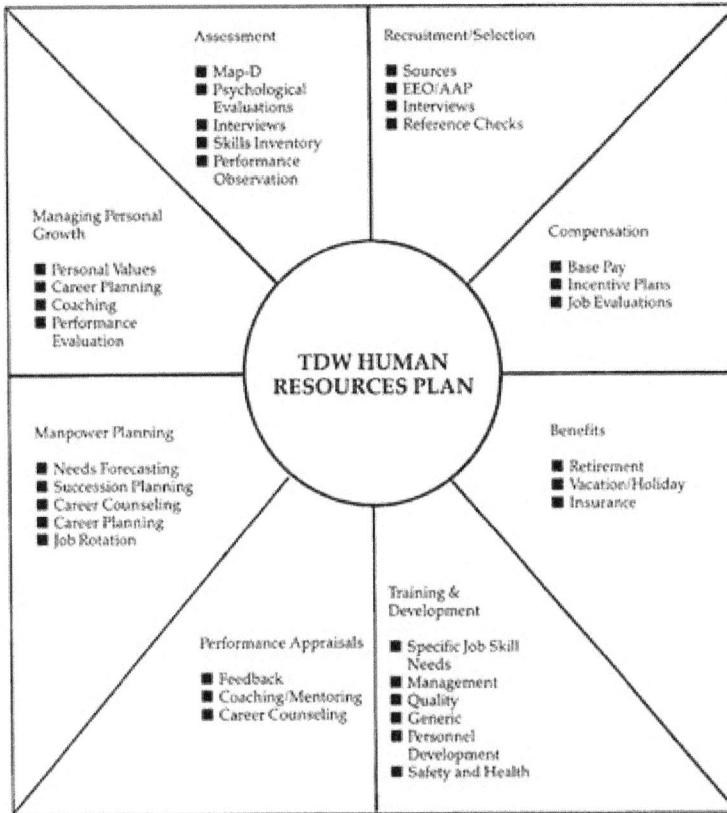

Assessment
- Map-D
- Psychological Evaluations
- Interviews
- Skills Inventory
- Performance Observation

Recruitment/Selection
- Sources
- EEO/AAP
- Interviews
- Reference Checks

Managing Personal Growth
- Personal Values
- Career Planning
- Coaching
- Performance Evaluation

Compensation
- Base Pay
- Incentive Plans
- Job Evaluations

TDW HUMAN RESOURCES PLAN

Manpower Planning
- Needs Forecasting
- Succession Planning
- Career Counseling
- Career Planning
- Job Rotation

Benefits
- Retirement
- Vacation/Holiday
- Insurance

Performance Appraisals
- Feedback
- Coaching/Mentoring
- Career Counseling

Training & Development
- Specific Job Skill Needs
- Management
- Quality
- Generic
- Personnel Development
- Safety and Health

After years of consulting work, I always notice that the human resources plan gets attention only after the corporate plan, marketing, production, and finance plans are in place. At this time I'm working with six firms on the development of human resources plans. In each of these cases the other plans are in place. All are using the model in this chapter. The major theme of the chapter is that the human resources top person must be involved in developing the overall strategic plan. With all my clients, I make sure the human resources function is represented. Unfortunately, in most organizations the human resources function finds out about the overall plan after it is developed. This is a tragic and all too often made mistake. Fellow consultant and friend Steve Haines has been a leader in the importance of human resources as a competitive advantage. I worked with Haines developing a fully integrated human resources plan for Imperial Corporation of California. Another company with a sophisticated five-year human resources plan is T. D. Williamson Inc., David Miller, Vice President of Human Resources, developed their human resources plan. The human resources plan fits into the overall firm's strategic plan. Note model one for the TOW plan. Also, note model developed by Stella M. Nkomo.

Figure 9.2
Human Resource Planning in Manufacturing Firms

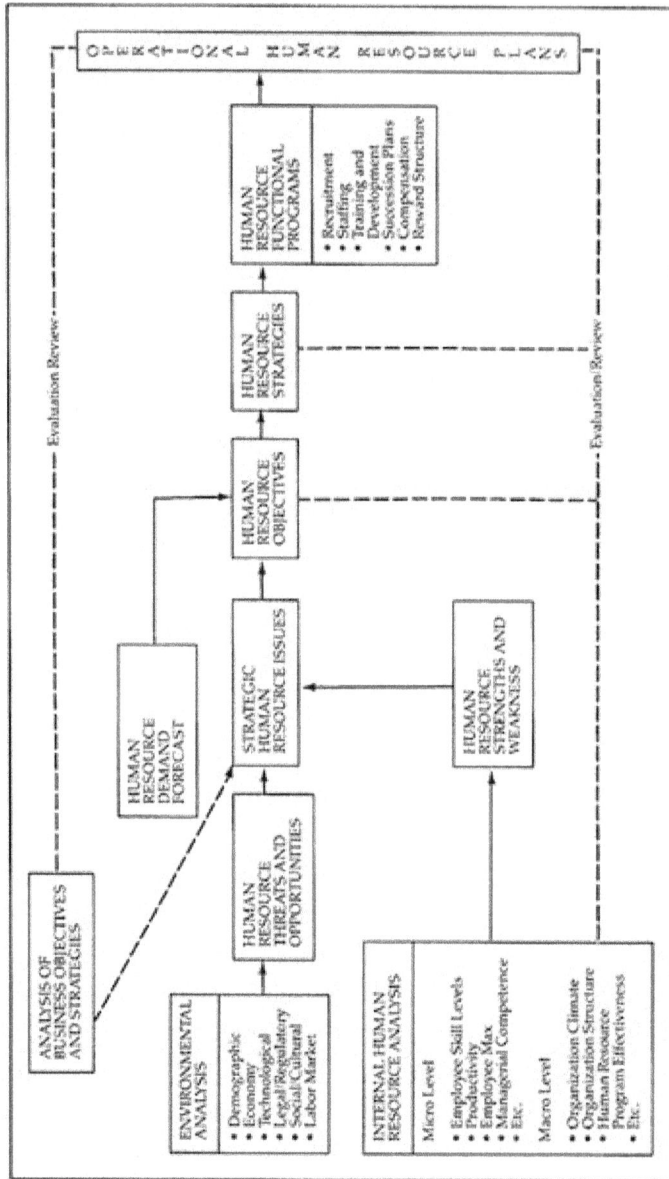

Anyone not convinced long-term human resources planning is needed might consider a few case histories. One large defense company bid on a big contract. To complete the project they needed specifically trained engineers. They got the contract and had difficulty hiring the engineers. A large multinational aluminum company had to scrap a big sophisticated computerized smelter in Brazil because there was no trained work force to operate the plant.

Any company responding to technological change needs to be planning for the inevitable changes in workforce composition and newly needed skills.

Figure 9.3
Long-Term Human Resources Planning

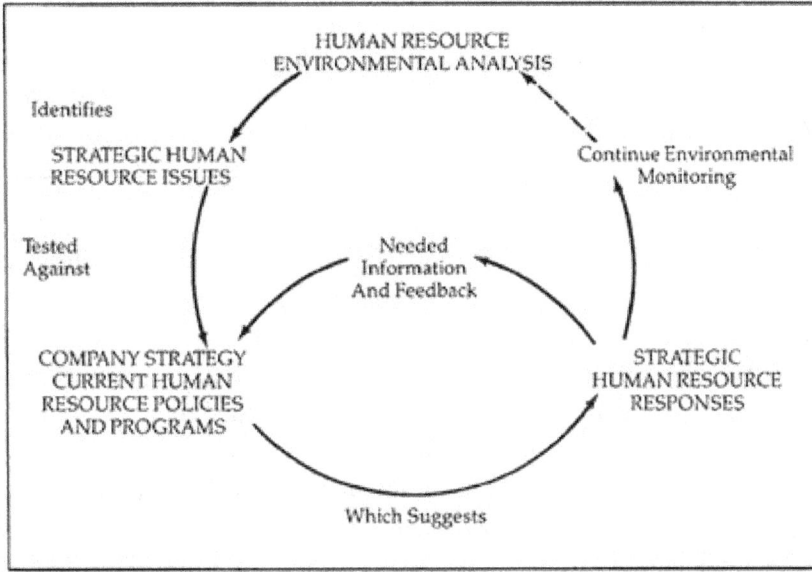

Level	Responsibility	Focus
Corporate	Corporate Human Resource Staff and Corporate Management	Organization wide human resource strategies and policies tailored to fit the corporate mission and business portfolio planning
Business/Division	Divisional Human Resource Staff and Division Management	Human resource strategies and policies tailored to meet specific product/market/customer segments
Department	Departmental Human Resource Staff	Human resource programs and policies for each functional area (e.g., recruitment, staffing, compensation, career development) etc.

Human Resource Strengths and Weaknesses	
Microanalysis Nature of the Workforce	Macroanalysis Organizational Context
• Employee demographics • Employee skill levels • Productivity and performance • Employee potential • Employee satisfaction • Management competence	• Organization climate • Organization structure • Quality of work life • Absenteeism trends • Turnover trends • Job analysis and job design • Cost/Benefit of current human resource programs

Much of the growth of the field of human resource planning parallels the growth of its broader human resources field. The human resource field has gone through various stages in its own evolution that can best be viewed by the changing terminology employed. One of the first terms used was "industrial relations." It dealt with the very rudimentary need to have a small workforce during the early stages of American industrialization. Later, the terms "labor relations" and "employee relations" were used depending on whether or not you were unionized (labor was the union term). As these functions became written into law and a profession began developing around these laws, the term "personnel administration" became popular. It often signified that the main purpose of the field was to administer the necessary paperwork to ensure employees were paid, had benefits coverage, and the firm complied with the increased requirements of the labor and EEO laws.

In the '50s and '60s, as the need to be concerned about employees increased, the term "human relations" came into vogue. It often meant that the firm wanted to be more parental towards its employees. Finally in the '70s and '80s, "human resources" has become the generally accepted term among progressive companies. Ideally, this has meant that the HR function, has become a full strategic partner in the business. In many instances, however, this has been an unfulfilled promise. Changing the terminology alone does not make human resource a strategic partner.

Unfortunately, the same terminology problem has held true for the field of Human Resource Planning. The field is rarely a bottom-line competitive business advantage for most organizations today, despite some claims to the contrary.

While the evolution of HRP may have been over the past half of this century, it was not widely acknowledged as a field until Eric Vetter defined it in 1967 as:

> ...the process by which management determines how the organization should move from its current manpower position

to its desired position. Through planning, management strives to have the right number and the right kinds of people, at the right places, at the right time, doing things which result in both the organization and the individual receiving maximum long-run benefits (as quoted in Fiorito 1982).

Early Development and Evolution of HR Planning

The above definition evolved out of the literature on manpower planning, the dominant form of what little personnel planning there was in the 1950s. Manpower planning in the 1950s was usually just the forecasting of numbers of employees needed to run next year's business. This concept wasn't much different from that espoused by economist Alfred Marshall back in 1890. He observed that "the head of a business must assure himself that his managers, clerks, and foremen are the right men for their work and are doing their work well." (quoted in Walker 1979).

Even into the 1970s and 1980s this manpower planning concept was the focus of popular articles in the HR literature (Berger 1976, Russ 1982). It was also the dominant focus of James W. Walker (1970-1971) considered by some to be the father of HRP. During this time frame one of the authors was personally exposed to firms such as TRW, General Electric and Marriott Corporation. They all used a similar process called manpower reviews as a key component in their personnel department's activities.

During the '70s, however, the terms "manpower" and "human resource" planning began to be used interchangeably (Walker 1973, Shaeffer 1976). It was indicative of a broadening focus for the field of HR planning. Allen Janger (1977) observed that the planning for the human resources of an organization was becoming more complex due to changing factors both external to, and within the corporation. These included items such as the changing environment, business strategies, growth and expansion as well as the demographics of the employees themselves. This complexity and the increased need for professionalism to deal with these issues drove the growth of this newer field of human resource planning.

In 1977, a professional society called The Human Resource Planning Society was formed, a sure sign that this fledgling field was growing. Positions for HRP specialists began to be found in the want ads and within Human Resource Departments. The authors believe that an accepted definition of HRP at this time might have seen it as a process of analyzing an organization's HR needs under changing conditions and developing the activities necessary to satisfy those needs. Thus, planning *and* developing programs to meet employee needs extended the previous more narrow view of manpower planning.

Edgar Schein (1977) was one of the first to embrace and extend this definition to include not only HR planning but "development" as well. Reid (1977) also reported on HRP at Xerox as "a tool for people development".

Differentiation in the Field of HR Planning

HRP began to have a number of practitioners differentiate their activities from their colleagues. Work force planning, for example (DeSanto 1983), was seen as an idea whose time had come. DeSanto felt work force planning would integrate decisions on the recruitment, development, and utilization of human resources into the overall system of corporate planning.

Annual HR planning also began to emerge as something that HR departments should do each year, just as one does annual corporate business planning.

Executive continuity and succession planning became other key concepts under the HRP umbrella (Mahler and Gaines 1983, Rhodes and Walker 1984).

The term "Management Resource Planning" was coined by Bolt (1982) for use at Xerox. It embodied this succession planning concept and extended the planning for replacements further down into the middle management ranks.

Areas such as "career planning and development" became associated under the HRP umbrella (Hall and Hall 1976), as did "performance appraisal," "performance improvement," and "performance management" (McFillen and Decker 1978).

At various times, other types of planning within the general functions of a human resource department were grouped under this new, almost faddish, concept of HRP. These HR plans included recruitment planning, merit planning, and affirmative action planning (AAP's) among others.

Finally, in order to further confuse the issue, training and development departments and HRP departments are often now called by a single new name, "Human Resource Development" (HRD). It appears this term is becoming a generally accepted one as the umbrella for the entire training and development field (see, for example, University Associates HRD '87 conference).

Current State of the Art in HR Planning

The critical need in the 1980s is for all of these various HRP activities to become more closely linked to the business and more relevant to senior management. While stated in various terms, all the needs expressed by these various types of planning techniques within the broadly defined human resource field have a common theme of becoming more business oriented.

One school of thought currently looks at HRP from the point of view of the entire human resources function needing to do strategic planning (Goodmeasure 1982; Devanna, Fombrun and Tichy 1980). They included such activities as defining "What should we be doing, and how can we successfully do it?" They also developed a topology of five specific activities that HR personnel should help line executives plan for:

1. Matching executives to strategic plans.
2. Defining long-run managerial characteristics of the firm.
3. Modifying rewards to encourage strategic objectives.
4. Changing staffing patterns to help implement strategies.
5. Appraising key personnel for their future roles in this (Devanna 1980).

Another school of thought about these issues comes from the field of organization design. It is embodied by Jay Galbraith (1973) who works backwards from business plans and strategies towards HRP with what he calls "organization planning". He sees this as more than structure alone. It also includes management processes, rewards, values and people (Galbraith 1986). Even the Planning Executives Institute has now begun to look at planning from a human resource viewpoint much as Galbraith has done (Kaumeyer 1984).

A third view (Miles and Snow 1985) focuses on designing strategic human resource "management systems" as the method for linking HR more to the business and its objectives.

Finally, some of the HRP practitioners themselves, through their HR Planning Society, have focused on the need to link HRP to the strategic plans of corporations. This Society has sponsored research in five major corporations regarding the status of HRP. It found both narrowly focused HRP programs with an emphasis on staffing as well as the more comprehensively focused HRP programs that were tightly linked to the main corporate strategic planning processes (Dyer 1986).

These comprehensive approaches included four key attributes: (1) a wide range of HR activities, (2) both a long and short range focus, (3) covered virtually the entire corporation's employees, and (4) had a formal planning process that looks at the environment, the business and the employees.

A number of other authors in the '80s have also looked at HRP from the point of view of integrating it with the organization's strategic plans (see Golle and Holmes 1984, Walker 1978, Ulrich 1986, Hennecke 1984, Kelleher and Cotter 1984).

George S. Odiorne sees the major tool of HRP to be the "environmental scan." He sees most HR strategic planning as being environmentally driven as opposed to just market driven. He also sees it organization-wide, multiyear in duration and producing significant changes in the character of the organization.

A Redefinition of HR Planning

While the above may represent the current state of the art in HRP, a further elevating of its importance is only being written about by a few futuristic authors. Gould (1984), Mills (1985), and Ulrich (1987) all discuss organizations gaining a competitive business advantage through their employees and doing strategic planning with their people in mind.

This is a newer school of thought that links employees and the business together with a consequence to both the bottom line of improved business profitability, along with improving the long term organizational health and viability. This is the author's basic definition of a competitive advantage:

> A competitive business advantage is that distinct and unique edge an organization has over its competitors and substitutes that:
>
> - The organization is known for, cannot be readily duplicated.
> - Can be renewed and viably sustained over a long period of time.
> - Results in a bottom-line organizational success and profitability greater than their average competitors over this time period.
> - While desired employees grow and thrive.

This competitive advantage notion may have a common sense appeal and face validity. However, it is relatively new ground for HRP and the behavioral sciences in general. They rarely have *explicitly* advocated people as a competitive business advantage. Despite being *implicit* in the value set of the field, it has not been one is which many authors have been comfortable advocating. The lack of valid quantifiable research data has been one key barrier to being more explicit about people as a competitive business advantage.

Instead, competitive business advantages have generally been seen as deriving from traditional business sources such as cost advantages, uniqueness of product, markets, customers or geography (see Porter 1980, 1985).

This article proposes a redefinition of the field of human resource planning to encompass this crucial competitive business advantage concept. Without this notion, the HRP field will continue to be absent from the room when the real strategic decisions of the firm get made. Hence:

> *Human Resource Planning* is that integral portion of the organization's strategic planning process...
>
> that deals with identifying, planning, monitoring and reporting on the attraction, motivation, development, reward and retention of desired employees...

and results in a sustainable bottom-line competitive business advantage along with the constant renewal of the organization's health, human spirit, and vitality.

This far-reaching definition of HRP is currently an ideal except for, perhaps, a few of the excellent companies in the recent management literature (see Peters, 1982, 1985; O'Toole 1981, 1985; Waterman 1987). However, to the majority of American companies, this common sense viewpoint that "people are our most important asset" remains an ideal rather than a proven reality. The implications of this gap present an enormous challenge to HR executives and HRP practitioners if they want to make their partnership with senior line management become a reality.

The enormous challenge, discipline and persistence involved in showing senior line management that human resource programs and practices can produce a competitive business advantage in the marketplace is not minimized by any means. This challenge is due to the fact that the ultimate ownership understanding and implementation of this concept (and the outputs of any strategic planning process) are the responsibility of line management.

However, research by Hay Associates, the Institute of Social Research at the University of Michigan, Schuster, and others (see Haines 1987) are now documenting the fact that paying attention to the human side of an organization does result in a competitive business advantage. Interesting enough, Porter (1987) is beginning to agree with this in his strategic planning research, as shown below.

Levels of Strategic Planning

The ability to discuss HRP as a competitive business advantage depends on the level of planning one is discussing. Porter, for example discusses some of these levels in his 1987 Harvard Business Review article. As adapted by the authors, there are actually four levels of business strategies for any organization (see Figure 9-4).

These include:

Level 1. Corporate Strategy, which is the buying and selling of assets representing businesses in which one desires to compete. Porter lists four (4) main corporate strategy alternatives as a result of his research on 33 large, prestigious U.S. companies from 1950-1986. These strategies include portfolio management, restructuring, transferring skills or sharing activities. He concluded that the track record of corporate strategies is dismal in that they have generally dissipated instead of created shareholder value.

Figure 9-4	
HUMAN RESOURCES ROLES IN BUSINESS STRATEGIES AND PLANS	
Business Strategy Levels	Hr Strategic Role
1. Corporate Strategy • Portfolio management (buy/sell assets) • Restructuring assets	1. People/Organization Placement • Industry characteristics (mission formulation) • Transferring employees • Sharing resources • Executive selection • Organization design • Values audit (executive vs. employees)
2. Business Unit Strategy (SBU) • Competitive strategies • Market • Product • Financial • Employee • Manufacturing • Miscellaneous	2a. Employee-Driven Strategies (create a competitive advantage through employees) • Quality • Customer service • Productivity • Selling Channels 2b. HR Involvement in any Potential Strategy • Environmental scanning • Performance/ gap audit
3. Functional Strategies • All functions • Tactical planning • Operational planning	3. Human Resource Strategies • Implementing corporate/SBU strategies • Organization success profile (OSP) of key systems/programs
4. Strategic Management • Implementation • Leadership • Persistence	4. Change/Transition Management • Transition technology • Organization models/fit • Organizational behavior/ assumptions • Organization development • Management training • Human resource development • Action-research • Unfiltered feedback/renewal • Executive advice
Source: Stephen G. Haines, 1988	

Level 2. Business Unit Strategy, or the familiar Strategic Business Unit (SBU) where specific competitive strategies are chosen. A list of competitive business strategies has been distilled from research in this area by one of the authors.

I.   PRODUCT STRATEGIES

    1. Product/service applications
    2. Product uniqueness
    3. Technology
    4. Patents

II.   MARKET STRATEGIES

    5. Geographic niche
    6. Customer segment
    7. Marketing effectiveness
    8. Large market share

III.   FINANCIAL STRATEGIES

    9. Low cost price leadership
    10. Economies of scale
    11. Capital structure
    12. Diversification

IV.   SPECIAL CIRCUMSTANCES

    13. Unique distribution channels
    14. Vertical integration
    15. Natural resources
    16. Production capacity

V.   EMPLOYEE DRIVEN

    17. Unsurpassed customer service
    18. Employee productivity
    19. High quality reputation
    20. Unique selling channels

Level 3. Functional Strategies, which include the planning for traditional functions such as finance, marketing, manufacturing, legal, data processing, human resources and the like. While this level of strategies goes by a number of different names such as tactical or operational planning, it is still a strategic set of decisions for the functional executive. It is this area that is most confusing within the HRP literature. Many authors and organizations who focus on HRP or "HR Strategic Planning" are really talking about this level of business planning, strategic from the point of view of the functional executive or department, but far different than the Corporate or SBU strategies of levels 1 and 2.

Level 4. Strategic Management, or implementation of all the strategies set at the higher levels 1, 2, and 3 above. This is the chaotic and difficult task of actually turning strategic plans into reality. It often requires changing an entire organization, a very difficult and time consuming task.

These four levels of strategy have enormous consequences for HR Planning. In order for HR Planning to become a bottom-line competitive business advantage, it must, by definition, be closely tied in some fashion to an organization's strategic planning process (as stated in the authors' redefinition of the field of HRP). The tying of HRP to the organization's strategy depends on what level of strategy one is dealing with, whether it is corporate, SBU, functional, or just strategic management and implementation.

In summary, the concept of strategic planning and the links of HRP to it are not as simple as one would like them to be in today's global world. It is now necessary to articulate the HRP linkages to each level of strategy.

Links to Level One: Corporate Strategy

At this highest level of strategy, the issue for the HR Executive is to understand and be a partner in the organization's complete corporate-wide strategic planning process. One of the more typical strategic planning processes is a model I first presented in 1974. It has since been refined over the years through positive study and work in the field of strategic planning (Migliore 1974, 1984, 1986, 1987, 1988). See Figure 9-5 for details. This model is being effectively used in a wide range of organizations, not only in the private sector, but also with nonprofit organizations such as hospitals, the public sector and ministries.

This process covered in earlier chapters and reviewed again here begins with an organization's purpose or mission, next goes through an environmental analysis, the strengths and weaknesses of the firm, and then all the way through the objectives, operational plans, evaluation and rewards. While this process is more fully described in the referenced texts, the role of the HR Executive as a partner in this strategic process depends on the strategy level with which one is involved.

To illustrate, at the Corporate strategy level, there are three main areas of focus for HR Planning. The first is the area of examining the structure and main characteristics of the industry under consideration in order to decide if the mission of the overall corporation should include doing business in this industry. For example, looking at the types and number of employees needed, along with their values compared to those of senior management, is crucial to determining whether the corporation's mission includes a particular industry.

Further, the demographics and the values of today's work force have changed dramatically over the past few years. Key issues include the baby boom, baby bust, aging population, employee rights, women in the work force, a greater number of Hispanics, etc. Yankelovich's *New Rules* (1981) has more information on this subject. However, the issue is clear, to determine what senior management is getting themselves in for by entering a particular industry.

Figure 9-5
Strategic Planning Process

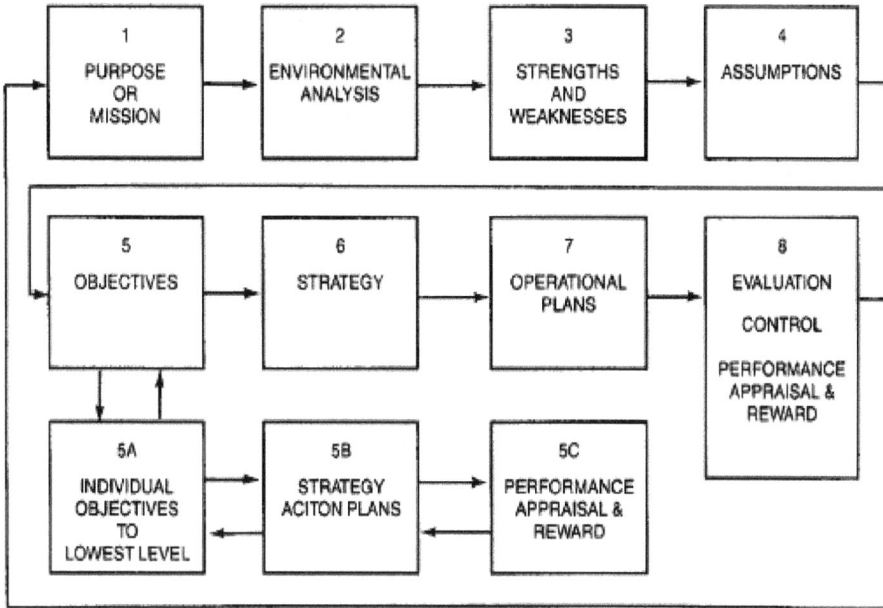

The second HRP area of corporate strategy focus is the arena of organization design. It is not just a given that the buying and selling of assets will result in the proper structure for the overall corporation. The understanding of the structural aspects of organizational theory may be unusual for HR Executives to learn, but they are essential. Designing organizations requires knowledge and skills in the areas of mission-strategy-structure linkages, integration and differentiation, centralization-decentralization, organization life cycles, work flow analysis and simplification, job design and its motivational impact, cost and impact analysis, slack resources, and sharing of resources. The issue here is not that one structure is correct but that they all have their strengths and weaknesses. Deciding which problems the senior management chooses to deal with as barriers to success is the real question.

The third areas of focus for an HR Executive during corporate strategy level deliberations is staffing. This includes executive selection, transferring employees into newly acquired business assets, and sharing of scarce employee resources. These activities are also advocated as priorities by Michael Porter (1987) in order to ensure a proper fit of the executives and other employees with the mission-strategy-structural analysis above. Despite much HR preoccupation with developing human resources, initial selection and job fit is still much more important to overall organizational success, especially at this level.

Links to Level Two: Business Unit Strategy

The HR Executive's issue of being involved in the strategic planning process at this level is similar and yet different from level one. It is similar in that the strategic planning *process* in Figure 9-5 is the same one at this level. However, from the 20 possible strategies an SBU might select, four of them are employee-driven strategies. These four are much more fundamentally dependent on employees to achieve success. They include quality, customer service, productivity, and selling channels (see Figure 9-6 for a graphic illustration).

Figure 9-6
Organization Goals and Employee Needs: A Unique Competitive Advantage

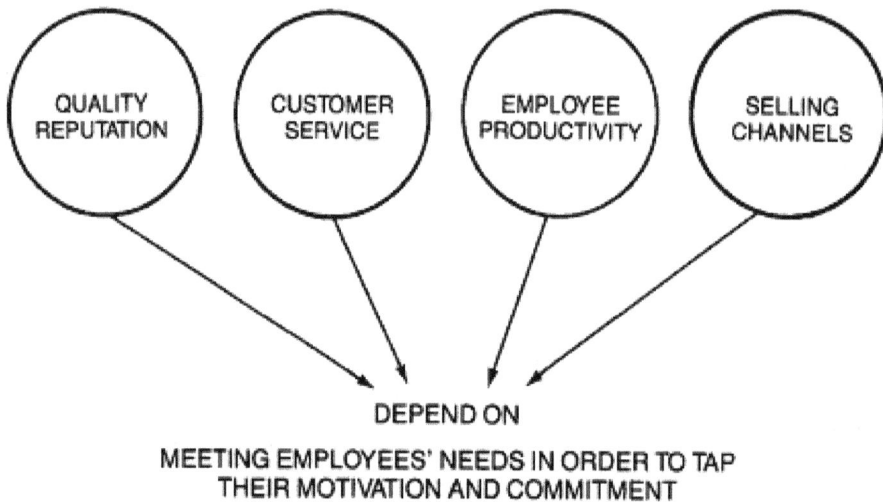

QUALITY REPUTATION   CUSTOMER SERVICE   EMPLOYEE PRODUCTIVITY   SELLING CHANNELS

DEPEND ON

MEETING EMPLOYEES' NEEDS IN ORDER TO TAP
THEIR MOTIVATION AND COMMITMENT

As an example, Ford Motor Company is known for its slogan of "Quality is Job One", and Chrysler for its seven-year, 70,000 mile warranty. Customer service is the hallmark of Marriott Corporation, McDonalds, and Nordstrom department stores. Productivity as a strategy is key to many Japanese firms. Their car manufacturers can produce a car for half the labor costs of U.S. auto manufacturers. Finally, Tupperware, Avon and encyclopedia companies are known for their unique selling channels.

In all of these employee-driven strategies, the involvement, knowledge, and skills of the professional HR Planner and others in HR associated fields are at the core of how to make these strategies succeed.

However, the HR Executive's involvement and role in the selection of the other non-employee driven strategy choices is also crucial. HR brings key information and expertise to the table during the phases of Figure 3's strategic planning process concerning (1) environmental analysis (or scanning), (2) strengths and weaknesses (or performance audits and gap analysis), as well as at the (3) mission or purpose formulation (including values audits). This is crucial to determining the final objectives, strategies and operational/tactical/functional plans later in the strategic planning process.

Links to Level Three: Functional Strategy

In actual practice over the years, there is a lack of coordination of the production, marketing and finance plans with overall corporate as well as SBU strategic planning processes. It was apparent that this same fundamental link to the strategies was needed for a firm's people plans regardless of the actual SBU and Corporate strategies chosen. In concept, all of these business functions and departments above should link to the overall corporate and SBU strategic plans in similar fashions.

In regards to HR Planning at this functional strategy level, it needs to occur in exactly the same manner and steps as the strategic planning process. HR Functional Plans must first define their purpose or mission. Next a scan of the external and internal environment must be accomplished, resulting in a diagnosing of the firm's people-related strengths and weaknesses. The rest of the planning steps follow.

Figure 9-7 shows this overall HR Planning process in detail and how it mirrors the strategic planning process noted in Figure 9-5.

Of special note, is the need to set clearly defined and measurable objectives just as executives do in finance, operations and the other business functions. Allowing soft and vague phrases such as "improve the productivity, morale, satisfaction, (or whatever) of our human resources" is no more acceptable here than in the other business functions.

There are many areas of the previously cited HR Planning definition where specific objectives can be developed. Each firm's HR planning process must have its senior executives select their own unique objectives that fit for them. However, in the experience of the authors, areas such as turnover, training, rewards for performance, benefits, compensation levels, wellness levels, survey results, internal advancement, manpower forecasts, recruiting costs, succession candidates, etc., are all examples of areas where firms have successfully set objectives.

Success in HRP must be measurable over both the short and long term. All members of the senior management and human resource staffs must be active participants in this objective-setting process. This is key if an organization is to achieve HR's maximum potential as a competitive business advantage. This is true regardless of the strategies chosen at the higher strategy levels 1 and 2.

Conclusion

Special attention here is necessary regarding two key factors usually missing from HR Planning. First, measures for the objective-setting and tracking of these "soft" areas are usually missing. However, the literature is now beginning to show that this area can be measured (Haines 1987). In addition, one of the authors did in fact set up an effective administrative MIS for all his areas of responsibility (including HR) while an executive vice president at Imperial Corporation of American, an $11 Billion asset-sized financial services company.

Second, the prominent place that the evaluation and control step in the strategic planning process plays in its ultimate success is often missing in the HR arena. Reviews of HRP progress by senior management are relatively uncommon in the authors' experiences. Yet, reviews of other traditional business functions (finance, operations, etc.) are usually held by senior management. The stewardship of the employees of the organization is no less important!

Methods to accomplish this review need to be decided early in the process of HRP. One of the most useful methods by firms such as IBM, EXXON, and others is the use of an annual survey feedback process (see Nadler 1977 for more information). In it, management receives unfiltered and quantifiable feedback on employees' perception of management's results regarding HR and business objectives.

As a result of recent research, it has become clearer that organizational and HR programs help constitute a bottom line competitive business advantage for firms (Haines 1987). Thus, the authors recommend the use of the Organizational Practices Profile (OPP) as an excellent vehicle to measure the status of their effectiveness in creating a competitive advantage through people (Haines 1987).

This OPP survey can be very effectively used to supplement other quantitative data collected on agreed upon HRP objectives. It is important here to note consistency with our redefinition of the HRP field to include its monitoring and reporting functions.

Cascio's1982 book entitled, *Costing Human Resources: The Financial Impact of Behavior in Organizations* makes fascinating reading on the bottom line competitive business advantage of HR functional level plans. Even Michael Porter (1987) found that the key to successful corporate-level strategies was the sharing of personnel resources or the transferring of executives and managers systematically across different corporate assets or entities. Again, functional HR plans can become competitive advantages regardless of the corporate strategy chosen.

Figure 9-7
Overall HR Planning Process
(as a Competitive Business Advantage)

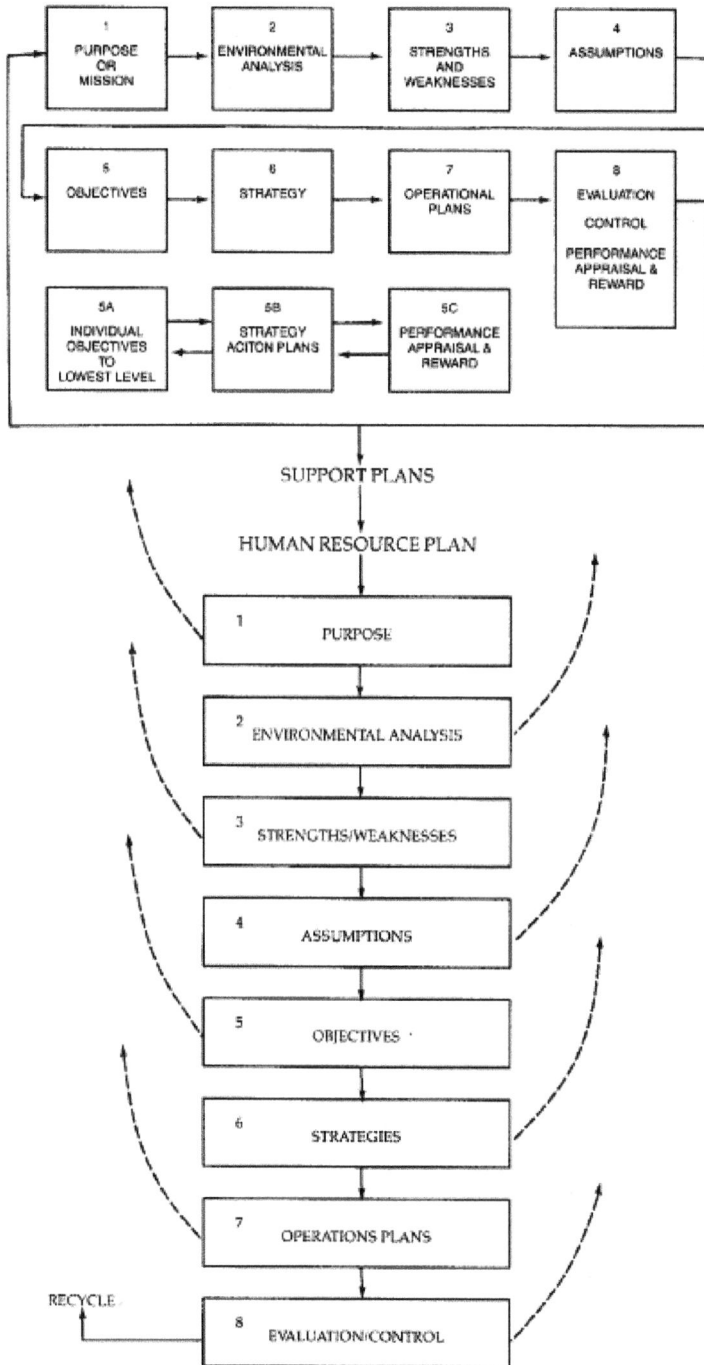

Note: Dashes tie in each step in the strategic planning process to the corresponding box of the human resources plan. This is key to the success of this process.

Level Four: Strategic Management

The strategic management and implementation of the HR plan is fraught with numerous barriers to success. Clearly, there are many ways an organization can achieve the same end result. Therefore, any HRP professional who approaches the CEO and senior management with the one best way is heading for potential trouble. The authors' HRP redefinition and framework may appear to be quite specific. However, the strategic management of change associated with implementing a strategic plan is dependent on many factors unique to each organization, its senior executives and the situation.

Some of the most important factors are the CEO's preferred leadership style, his or her level of implementation persistence, the firm's culture or norms of behavior, and the existing political realities.

There is obviously a key role that the HR Planner (and the entire HR Department) can play in implementing the plan. First, there are a number of skills and concepts that must be acquired.

These include:

1. The entire area of transition and change management technology (see Beckhard 1977).

2. A diagnostic model/methodology on how to view an organization as an overall system (see Galbraith 1973, 1977).

3. The ability to serve as a highly professional adviser and consultant to senior executives.

4. The facilitator and process skills of the organization's development professionals.

As stated, it is beyond the scope of this chapter to delineate the specific change or transition steps needed for each unique situation. Nevertheless, the kinds of issues and barriers to be encountered along the way to strategically managing the implementation process are relatively common. Some of the more recent articles that highlight these barriers include Rowland (1981), Mackey (1981), Leskin (1984), and Burack (1985). For ease of presentation, they are grouped into two categories, strategy formulation (i.e. Business Strategy Levels 1-2-3) and strategy management and implementation (Level 4).

Strategy Formulation Barriers:

1. Lack of a champion.

2. The skills, business acumen, and credibility of the vice presidents of both human resources and the planning function.

3. No clear sense of the vision and strategic direction of the overall firm.

4. Inability of the HR head to be involved.

5. Lack of a close tie-in between HR and corporate planning.

6. Not having senior management committed at every level of the strategic plan.

7. Letting staff develop any level of strategic plans.

8. Inadequate environmental assessment of future trends.

9. Confusing budgeting with planning.

10. Failure to think comprehensively about those HR programs and practices that will motivate the firm's employees to become a competitive business advantage.

Strategy Implementation Barriers

1. The culture of any organization is both its strength and its limitation

2. The conflict the plan causes with the organization's political minefields

3. Failure to continually communicate fully throughout the process of implementation

4. In addition, failure to gather feedback on the plan's status, acceptance, and motivational impact is like an out of control satellite. Without feedback, midcourse corrections are rarely successful.

5. Despite the best intent of senior management, a crucial barrier to success is the fact that many organizations have two distinct and different cultures: management and nonmanagement! A clear understanding of the nonmanagement culture and their needs and desires is necessary to properly target the HR Plan. The title to a long forgotten article makes the point: "If it's right for you, it's wrong for your employees!"

6. The correctness of an HR plan is subject to the traditions of the human resources field. Unfortunately, many of the traditional solutions in the HR field are ones formulated in a different era than the 1980s. While they may have met the unique needs of the employees of that 1940s and 50s era, old guideposts are often the wrong solutions today (see Haines 5/1987 for specific examples). Proven research on what works in the field of human and organizational behavior is frequently ignored by HR and line executives, resulting in a strong negative impact on the success of the HR Plan.

7. Rewards systems are always crucial to the successful implementation of any plans and programs. Careful recrafting of all parts of a total rewards system (both financial and nonfinancial) to fit faithfully with all aspects of the four levels of strategic plans is absolutely essential.

This lack of fit is where most strategic management and implementation plans go awry.

8. Not monitoring the progress of the plans on a regular basis.

9. HR policies, programs and practices are fragmented among different specialists.

Summary

This redefinition of HR Planning has the potential to be one of the ways an organization can develop its competitive business advantage. Recognition is coming slowly. Employees can drive the selection of both a corporate and a business unit strategic plan. It is becoming more understood by senior management that their employees hold the keys to successful strategic management and implementation. This is regardless of the specific strategy chosen. Perhaps this is due to more and more firms choosing their competitive advantages in the employee-driven areas of (1) customer service, (2) cost efficiencies and productivity, (3) unique selling channels or (4) quality products. The one thing these four strategies have in common is the dependency on meeting employees' needs in order to tap their futll motivation and commitment to act in support of these strategies. Employees can also support or block implementation of a well thought out strategic plan, and especially so in these four cases.

This redefinition of HRP is more an ideal than reality in most organizations today. However, it is still a vision for HR executives to strive for in order to be taken more seriously and successfully by senior executives. The latest data available indicates there are few organizations with fully developed five-year human resource plans. It is becoming clearer through Porter's research and case studies of the failures of People's Express and MCI Communications that price or costs alone do not result in a long-term competitive business advantages. They are only half a loaf, necessary, but not sufficient for long-term success.

While the concepts, perils and challenges of HR planning are great for the HR professional, so are the potential rewards! By having the H.R. function represented when strategic direction is set, the organization is more likely to have a fully developed H.R. plan.

Human Resources Plan

	Last Year Actual	Next Year	Five Years
Culture Index			
Yearly People Development Audit			
Quality Circles (participation teams) implemented			
Turnover			
Performance/Reward System			
Benefits			
Compensation Levels			
Wellness			
Manpower Forecast			
Recruiting Objectives and Costs			
Succession Planning			
Affirmative Action			
Pro-Active Labor Relations			
Culture Index			
Measure of Skills Needed/100 Index			
Full Time/Temporary Employee Ratios			
Cross Training Index			
Literacy Rate			
Computer Literacy			
Legislation			

References

Beckhard, R., Harris, R. *Organization Transition: Managing Complex Change*. Reading. MA: Addison-Wesley. 1977.

Berger, L. "Dispelling a Mystique: Practical Managerial Manpower Planning" *Personnel Journal*. June 1976:296-299.

Bolt, J. "Managing Resource Planning: Keys to Success" *Human Resource Planning* 1982:185-195.

Burack, E. "Corporate Business and Human Resources Planning Practices: Strategic Issues and Concerns" *Organizational Dynamics*. 1984:73-87.

Burack, E. "Linking Corporate Business and Human Resource Planning: Strategic Issues and Concerns" *Human Resource Planning*. 1985:133-146.

Cascio, W. *Costing Human Resources: The Financial Impact of Behavior in Organizations*. Boston, MA: Kent Publishing 1982.

DeSanto, J. "Work Force Planning and Corporate Strategy" *Personnel Administrator*. October 1983:33-36.

Devanna, M.A., Fombrun, C.J, & Tichy. N. M. *Human Resource Management: A Strategic Approach*. Unpublished manuscript. Columbia University. Graduate School of Business. New York. 1 February 1980.

Dyer, L. "Human Resource Planning at IBM" *Human Resource Planning*. 1984: 111-126.

Dyer, L. (Ed.). *Human Resource Planning: Tested Practices Five Major U.S. and Canadian Companies*. New York: Random House 1986.

Dyer, L., Shafer, R., & Regan, P. "Human Resource Planning at Corning Glass Works: A Field Study" *Human Resource Planning*. 1982:115-184.

Fiorito, J. "The Rationale for Human Resource Planning" *Human Resource Planning*. 1982:103-104.

Fraze, J. "Displaced Workers: Okies of the 80s" *Personnel Administrator,* January 1988:42-56.

Galbraith, J. *Designing Complex Organizations*. Reading, MA: Addison Wesley. 1973.

Galbraith, J. *Organization Design*. Reading, MA: Addison-Wesley, 1977.

Galbraith, J. (Speaker). *Organization Planning*. Imperial Corporation of America. San Diego, CA. November 1986.

Gould, R. "Gaining a Competitive Edge Through Human Resource Strategies" *Human Resource Planning*. 1984:32-38.

Hall, D., & Hall, F. "What's New in Career Management" (Reprint). *Organizational Dynamics*, Summer 1976:191-214.

Haines, S. *Organizational Rewards: Why Don't We Use What Works?* Speech presented at The Center for Effective Organizations, University of Southern California, Los Angeles. May 1987.

Haines, S. *Human Resources as a Competitive Business Advantage* (Doctoral Proposal). Temple University, Philadelphia, Pennsylvania. 1987.

Hennecke, M. "The "People" Side of Strategic Planning" *Training* November 1984:25-31. *Human Resource Planning: Strategy Formulation and Implementation*. Minnetonka, MN: Golle & Holmes Consulting 1984.

Janger, A. *The Personnel Function: Changing Objectives and Organization* (Report No. 712). New York: The Conference Board, 1977.

Kaumeyer, R., Jr. *Human Resources: A Critical Planning Issue*. Oxford, OH: Planning Executives Institute. 1984.

Kelleher, E., & Cotter, K. "An Integrative Model for Human Resource Planning and Strategic Planning" *Human Resource Planning* 1982:15-16. Leskin, B. Human Resources Strategic Planning. Paper presented at the meeting of CEO Sponsor's Group, Los Angeles: CA, 5 May 1984. Mackey, C. "Human Resource Planning: A Four-Phased Approach". *Management Review*, May 1981:17-21.

Mahler, W., & Gaines, F. Jr., *Succession Planning in Leading Companies*. Midland Park, NJ: Author, 1984.

McFillen, J., & Decker, P. "Building Meaning into Appraisal" (Reprint). *The Personnel Administrator*, June 1978: 23(6).

Migliore, R. *MBO: Blue Collar to Top Executive*. Washington, D.C.: BNA Press 1974.

Migliore, R. *An MBO Approach to Long Range Planning*. Englewood Cliffs, NJ: Prentice Hall, 1984.

Migliore, R. *Strategic Long Range Planning* (rev. ed.). Tulsa, OK: Western Printing, 1986.

Migliore, R., Spence, J., & Thurn, W. *Production Operations Management: A Productivity Approach*. Jenks, OK: J. Williams, 1987.

Miles, R., & Snow, C. "Designing Strategic Human Resources Systems" *Organization Dynamics*, 1983:36-52.

Mills, D. "Planning with People in Mind*" Harvard Business Review*, July-August 1985:97-105.

Nadler, D. *Feedback and Organization Development: Using data-based methods*. Reading, MA: Addison-Wesley, 1977.

Nkomo, S.M. "Strategic Planning for Human Resources-Let's get Started," *Long Range Planning*, 2(1), 1988: 66-72.

Odiorne, George S. (personal communication). Eckerd College, St. Petersburg, FL August 31, 1987.

O'Toole, J. *Making America Work: Productivity and Responsibility*. New York: Continuum, 1981.

Peters, T., & Waterman, R., Jr. *In Search of Excellence: Lessons from America's Best-Run Companies*. New York: Harper-Row, 1982.

Peters, T., & Austin, N. *A Passion for Excellence: The Leadership Difference*. New York: Random House 1985.

Pfeiffer, W. (Ed.). *Strategic Planning: Selected Readings*. San Diego, CA: University Associates, 1986.

Pfeiffer, J. W., Ph. D., J. D. *Power and Organizational Politics: Managing the Change Process*. La Jolla, CA: University Associates, 1987.

Porter, M. *Competitive Strategy*. New York: The Free Press, 1980.

Porter, M. *Competitive Advantage: Creating and Sustaining Superior Performance*. New York: The Free Press, 1985.

Porter, M. "From Competitive Advantage to Corporate Strategy" *Harvard Business Review*, May-June 1987:45-59.

Reid, D. "Human Resource Planning: A Tool for People Development" *Personnel* March-April1977:15-25.

Rhodes, D., & Walker, J. "Management Succession and Development Planning;' (Reprint). *Human Resource Planning* 1984:7(4).

Rowland, K., & Summers, S. "Human Resource Planning: A Second Look" *Personnel Administrator*, December 1981:73-80.

Russ, C., Jr. "Manpower Planning Systems: Part II" *Personnel Journal*. February 1982:119-123.

Schein, E. "Increasing Organizational Effectiveness Through Better Human Resource Planning and Development;' (Reprint). *Sloan Management Review* Fall1977:1-20.

Shaeffer, R. *Monitoring the human resource system*. Paper presented at The Conference Board's Division of Management Research. New York. 20 April 1976.

Strategic Planning for Human Resources. Cambridge, MA: Goodmeasure,1982.

Ulrich, D. "Human Resource Planning as a Competitive Advantage." *Human Resource Planning* 9(2), 1986: 41-50.

Ulrich, D. "Strategic Human Resource Planning: Why and How" *Human Resource Planning*, 10, (1), 1987:37-56.

Walker, J. "Problems in Managing Manpower Change" (Reprint). *Business Horizons* February 1970, pp. 63-68.

Walker, J. "Models in Manpower Planning" (Reprint). *Business Horizons* April1971:87-96.

Walker, J. Evaluating the practical effectiveness of human resource planning applications. Paper presented at the 20th International Meeting, Institute of Management Sciences, Tel Aviv, Israel, 24-29 June 1973.

Walker, J. "Linking Human Resource Planning and Strategic Planning" (Reprint). *Human Resource Planning*, 1(1), 1978:101-111.

Walker, J. "Human Resource Planning: An Evolution" (Reprint). Pittsburgh Business Review, 47(1), 2-8 March 1979.

Waterman, R., Jr. *The Renewal Factor* New York: Bantam, 1987. Yankelovich, D., *New Rules*. New York: Random House, 1981.

CHAPTER 10
STRATEGIC MANAGEMENT

The management team must guide the organization through the process of attaining the objectives outlined in the strategic plan. Part of the job is to stay within the philosophical and ethical boundaries of the purpose statement. Strategic management implies the management team will find the best uses for available resources. It will find the best culture for the organization to succeed and maintain that culture.

For example, one of my clients in Florida is a young aggressive computer service company. They have revenue and ROI objectives to double in next five years. Their mission statement reflects a strong commitment to ethics and integrity. Because of the creativity needed for new products and services the culture needed is one that encourages innovation. The president must balance the need for innovation with the need to control an expanding organization. The management philosophy must balance a business manager, secretaries, and telephone operator that work from 9:00 to 5:00 p.m., while R and D engineers and computer specialists work by inspiration.

Another part of strategic management is problem-solving. How do you handle the steady stream of major and minor problems? Years of helping other people solve problems has taught me a valuable lesson and approach. You must evaluate each situation in respect to its effect on where the organization wants to be in the long run. What people tend to think of as immediate, severe problems needing top management attention often have little effect on long term success. In that case the problem gets delegated down into the organization.

One manufacturing client of mine has achieved steady growth and has successfully reached initial revenue and return on investment objectives. At a recent planning retreat as we worked on 1995 objectives, it became apparent to everyone that major and/or minor problems depended on the long-term targets. Doubling of revenues presented one set of problems. If the long-term objectives were to maintain the present revenue and probability base, that meant grappling with another set of problems.

A recent experience illustrates the point. My work and travel schedule keeps my calendar full 12 to 18 months in advance. Two Texas churches had been seeking my assistance. An east coast trip was canceled at the last minute (environmental factor and assumption changed.) This created the opportunity for a fast two-day swing through San Antonio and College Station,

Texas. *Objective* was set to work one evening and one day with each church. *Objective* for both was to work with their management team to develop a rough draft plan up through objectives and then confront the major problems they perceived would prevent them from reaching the long-term objectives. They, like all organizations I work with, used the worksheet in Appendix A. Through gathered information (which is environmental analysis), it was apparent that regularly scheduled airlines wouldn't meet the needed arrival and departure times. Private aircraft was the best way to go (strategy). The whole operation was based on the *assumption* there would be good weather. Every assumption needs a *contingency plan.* I mailed the worksheet in Appendix A, a video training tape, and books ahead to both clients. Also, I discussed with a key person at each location what to do in case of delay.

Sure enough, we got about halfway to San Antonio and air traffic control closed Dallas-Ft. Worth airport due to weather conditions. They advised all small aircraft to land somewhere immediately. We did. We were on the ground for three hours. One simple phone call to the contact person, a fast review, and the meeting went on as scheduled. We flew in late that night after the weather cleared and had a very successful meeting. As we got set to leave San Antonio for the evening meeting in College Station, the same thing happened again— bad weather, one phone call, and a successful evening meeting. We flew in later when the weather cleared. I was away from home about 52 hours, traveled almost 2,000 miles, and helped two groups through the planning and problem identification process. The key point is to have a well thought-out plan, and then strategically to manage the plan.

If you have no plan, then you don't know what to manage. People rally around targets and directions. They need to know where the organization is going. It is top management's job to get them in on the plan.

Another key to problem solving is to develop at least three alternatives for each major and/or minor problem. All too often, not enough time is spent evaluating what the real problem is. Once the real problem is identified, then the various alternative courses of action must be determined.

Only by listing and discussing the alternatives can you set the stage to make the best choice of alternatives.

For example, on the trip to San Antonio we had a problem: bad weather. Another problem was the need to work with the client. Fortunately, with the contingency plan in effect the client's problem of getting the meeting going was minimized. The alternatives from that remote airport 60 miles from Dallas were:

1.   Call my wife and have her drive to pick us up and drive all night to San Antonio

2. Hire one of the workers there at the airport repair shop to drive us in an old pickup to Dallas for a commercial flight

3. Fly back to Tulsa and take a commercial flight to San Antonio the next day.

4. Wait a few hours and see if the weather improved. We chose the fourth alternative, arrived at San Antonio, had a good night's sleep, and worked the next day.

This problem-solving formula that, first of all, is based on where the organization is going, defining the real problem, and then developing all reasonable alternatives before making a choice has paid off in my work for years. This is what I call strategic management.

Another important aspect of strategic management is continuous improvement. Continuous improvement is driven by the philosophy in the purpose statement. The culture of the organization sets the tone for continuous improvement. Strategic management is the process and action of managing the strategic plan. If copies of the strategic plan are near at hand and have a few coffee stains with markings and notes, then the plan is being strategically managed. If the plan is on the shelf gathering dust, this suggests managing the same old way.

Chapter 11
Appraisals, Rewards, and Re-Evaluation

This chapter presents the concepts of appraisal systems, rewards, revision of objectives, and reevaluation. The objectives of this chapter are to understand the factors involved in appraisal, to appraise last year's performance, and to determine appropriate rewards if objectives, both intrinsic and extrinsic, are met. Also, you should be able to defend the reasoning for including reevaluation in the Long-Range Planning/MBO process.

Appraisal

The last stage in MBO is to appraise the organization and each of its entities to determine if all objectives have been met. Have the measurable objectives and goals been accomplished? How far did actual performance miss the mark? Did the attainment of the objectives and goals support the overall purpose? Has the environment changed enough to change the objectives and goals? Have additional weaknesses been revealed that will influence changing the objectives of the organization? Have additional strengths been added, or has your position improved sufficiently to influence the changing of your objectives?

Has the organization provided its members with organizational rewards, both extrinsic and intrinsic? Is there a feedback system to help the members satisfy their high-level needs? Please notice how my brand of Long-Range Planning/MBO is easily revised. Notice the various objectives and the quarterly review. If there is a deviation, the problem is red-flagged and given attention. For example, when I was Dean of the School of Business, I reviewed the School of Business objectives and results with my boss at the end of each semester and at the end of the summer. If there is a major problem that would inhibit goal attainment, I let him know immediately.

Part of the appraisal process is the reward system. Most organizations do not directly tie objectives and results to pay. I believe this is a mistake. It is my feeling that almost all the performance appraisal systems in use in this country are a waste of time and actually contribute to negative results. Harry Anderson recently reported on the problems.

> A recent report by the Conference Board noted that over half of the 293 firms it surveyed had developed new systems within the past three years. But despite these efforts, the report concludes, "current systems are still widely regarded as a nuisance at best and

a dangerous evil at worst." The latest rage in appraisal systems is something called "management by objectives" or MBO, which is used by over half the firms surveyed by the Conference Board. Under this system, an employee and his supervisor periodically sit down to negotiate what the subordinate should accomplish by the end of the rating period. A salesman, for example, might agree to increase new orders for his product by ten percent, while a production engineer could agree to hold manufacturing costs even. The employee's performance is then measured by how well he has met his predetermined objectives.

I have been through that process many, many times after having been on both sides of the fence. All that rating of poise, getting along with fellow workers, and so on is not the basis of a reward system. It is the negotiated results contracted between the individual and his boss. The traditional factors can then be covered with appraisal. The appraisal process is something that is difficult to manage. To determine if the organizational reward system is working properly, ask any member this question, "What is the most satisfying thing you do?" If the respondent lists half a dozen items and his work is not included, then you have an organizational problem. People are seeking the satisfaction of the higher level needs of self-esteem, recognition, and autonomy. I have administered the questionnaire in Chapter 7 to more than fifty organizations. The top-ranked job goals have been achievement, recognition, and opportunity for independent thought and action. If the organization does not have the means of satisfying these higher level needs, organizational members will go outside the organization to have these needs met. When this happens, the outside areas of interest, Girl Scouts, PTA, church clubs, and so on receive the major part of the enthusiasm, as well as the independent and innovative work of the organization member. His or her job, and the organization itself, receive only base efforts. An organization can sustain itself for quite a while in such a situation. The loss is hard to measure. What could have been accomplished if every organization member were receiving at least some of his or her satisfaction of high-level needs from within the organization and giving the resultant enthusiastic support to the organization?

I do not claim to understand this complex situation thoroughly, but I can make these observations:

1.   Salary is largely a dissatisfaction. If it is adequate, it tends to be a short-term motivator. If it is inadequate, it is a long-term problem and cuts down on innovative, enthusiastic support.

2.   Most people feel they are worth more than they are paid.

3. A universal problem in all industries and organizations is how to give extrinsic rewards for performance.

4. Provision must be made for the person to satisfy higher level needs within the organization.

5. Loyalty has ranked and will continue to rank high as a factor in the appraisal process.

Odiorne lists and explains 33 rules in "MBO Special Report; Compensation." A few of the more important are the following, using Odiorne's numbering:

2. Salary administration should be centered around accountability, not activity.

3. Write job objectives instead of job descriptions.

9. People who are committed to your organization are worth more than people who are not committed to it.

13. People who feel they are underpaid will behave like underpaid employees.

16. People who aren't meeting all of their regular ongoing and recurring responsibilities should not be given merit increases.

19. Bonuses should be paid only for beating an indicator.

23. Paying people below equitable market rates will assure you of an ironclad grip on marginal performance.

29. Fair pay does not motivate, but unfair pay demotivates.

31. The higher the person is in the organization, the more you pay for strategies and creative thinking.

Important for a proper appraisal system are the new legal trends and ramifications. Judges in several recent cases in California have looked hard at appraisal systems. They indicate that the appraisal system must be relevant and important to the job, not to some other standards such as personality or education. I can't think of anything safer, easier to understand, or more relevant than basing performance appraisal/pay/promotion on results achieved against agreed-on objectives.

Chuck Adams, when he was personnel manager for the City of Tulsa, developed an appraisal system with a system to rate and tie in rewards based on achieved results. It is well thought out. He has developed a point value that considers percentage of completion, effectiveness, and other factors that give an overall performance rating. This is then translated into a salary recommendation. I have, however, had difficulty with appraisals that are numbers and that are index-oriented.

Richard Jarvis, a financial executive with Red Cross and former Coordinator of Long-Range Planning at T. D. Williamson, Inc., used ideas he picked up from the Brunswick Appraisal System. He developed some innovative ideas of his own to better quantify the appraisal process.

Richard B. Higgins found in a recent study conducted among Fortune 1000 companies that those managers who were rewarded for their contributions to strategic planning believed they were doing a better job of planning, were more satisfied with their participation in the process, and were more positive about the results achieved by strategic planning. Simply stated, this tells us if we want good strategic planning, build it into the reward system.

Conclusion

After 25 years of organization consulting, it is my observation that those organizations that do the best job in the area of appraisal, rewards and reevaluation have a more stable, higher motivated work force. A more productive people factor gives that organization a competitive edge.

Performance Appraisal: An MBO Approach

The keys to performance appraisal and salary administration are profit and performance. This discussion focuses on two factors: (1) appraisal and reward for individual performance, and (2) group bonus reward systems.

Figure 11-1 shows the various possible reward alternatives each individual faces. In the lower left-hand section A, the low performer in an organization whose objectives were not achieved would receive low pay and a low bonus. At the other extreme in Section C, the individual had achieved his objectives and the organization had achieved its objectives; the individual would receive high pay and a high bonus. Alternatives B and D represent other situations. In B, the individual achieves his objectives, yet the organization has modest success. Thus, he receives high pay and a medium bonus. Alternative D is a situation in which a person didn't do as well at achieving his individual objectives but the organization did well, and he would receive medium pay and a high bonus. The rest of the chapter dis cusses specific programs that contribute to individual rewards along with the group bonus reward.

Ideally, the organization meets its broad overall purpose and reason for being. Specific measurable objectives in key result areas are largely met on a constant, sustaining basis. This success is based on a management team that has the motivation, ability, and insight to manage the organization's resources.

The individual manager meets or exceeds his specific, measurable, key result objectives.

	Reward Opportunities	
Individual Objectives Attained	High Pay (B) Medium Bonus	High Pay (C) High Bonus
	Low Pay (A) Low Bonus	Medium Pay (D) High Bonus

1	2	3	4	5	6	7	8	9	10

Organization Objectives Attained

The succetssful organization rewards its contributors: stockholders, owners, managers, and employees. As a spin-off, it now contributes to society in its roles as taxpayer, employer, and so on. It encourages its suppliers to make long-term plans to meet its needs. The ripple effect of success works its way down.

	Excellent 5	Above Average 4	Average 3	Below Average 2	Poor 1	Discussion Notes
1. Operate within budget of $146,032 and cost per credit hour of $130	5					
2. Graduate 25 MBAs in May 1980	5					
3. Maintain enrollment of 100 FTE MBA students		4				
4. Publish in top ½ of the nation	5					
5. Average 35 aerobic points per week and reduce weight to 205			3			
	15	4	3			22 = Total
1. Use of LRP/MBO	5					
2. Developing people	5					
3. Contribution to morale	5					
4. Communication			3			
5. Creativity	5					
6. Emotional stability	5					
7. Job knowledge		4				
8. What kind of leader	5					
9. Problem solver			3			
10. Public image	5					
	35	4	6			45 = Total

Average of objectives = 22 ÷ 5 = 4.4
Average of other items = 45 ÷ 10 = 4.5
Weighted average = (4.4 × 75%) + (4.5 × 25%) = 4.425

The successful organization now must devote attention to rewarding its own managers and employees for their contributions. The organization's needs are met. Now, how does the *organization* meet the extrinsic and intrinsic needs of its *people?*

The extrinsic needs have always been more difficult to deal with. Few salary and bonus systems do well over the long run. The big question mark among MBO scholars, students, consultants, and executives is: "How do you combine MBO with salary administration?"

This chapter deals with that subject. In its simplest form, the person must be evaluated on how he or she performed against key objectives that were negotiated, thoughtfully considered, and obtainable. The objectives are usually scored on a scale from 5 to 10.

The managers should also be evaluated. Then each year's pay increase should be based on performance of the 5 to 10 key performance objectives and the 10 criteria listed below:

1. Use of Long-Range Planning/MBO

2. Developing people

3. Contribution to morale

4. Communication

5. Creativity

6. Emotional stability

7. Job knowledge

8. Leadership style

9. Problem-solving ability

10. Public image/social responsibility

I have devised a method that takes already existing sets of objectives and turns them into appraisal forms. See Figure 11-2. The individual's regular performance objectives are listed at the top of the sheet, and their final outcome is given a rating of 5 for excellent through 1 for poor performance. The ten items previously listed are then rated according to the same system.

These ten items are not measurable, but they should be considered. I feel that the main criteria should be the results of how the managers performed as compared to what they negotiated as their performance objectives. Each objective at year end would be rated excellent through poor on performance. Table 11-1 could be followed in determining the specific pay increases. Average the objectives and give them a 75 percent weight, and give the 10 nonmeasurable areas a 25 percent weight.

If the person has fared well against these expectations and the organization has done well, he or she should receive a salary boost commensurate with the performance. In today's economic climate, this would be a 12 to 20 percent increase in pay.

Next, let's consider another circumstance: the organization doesn't do as well but the individual performer posted a good record in all areas over which he has control. He should be paid by the same criteria. The organization has too much at stake to risk losing its high performers. Usually 20 percent of the people contribute 80 percent of the key results. Don't be niggardly with the 20 percent The same rule of thumb, 12 percent to 20 percent pay increase, holds if the organization does poorly. The other 80 percent receive pay in the third 10 percent range.

Table 11-1

Performance Level	Recommended Pay
1. Performance less than satisfactory (has not met all minimum acceptable performance standards and objectives for the position). Point average below 1.5.	Zero percent increase
2. Performance meets minimum standards and objectives but not up to average. Point average 1.5 to 2.5.	Not more than 5 percent increase (0-5).
3. Performance meets at least average standards and objectives and may excel in some areas. Point average 2.5 to 3.5.	Not more than 10 percent increase (5-10).
4. Performance is better than average overall and excels in a majority of standards and objectives for the position. Point average 3.5 to 4.5.	Not more than 15 percent increase (11-15).
5. Performance is outstanding because it excels in all the objectives and conditions previously listed. Point average 4.5 to 5.0.	Not more than 20 percent increase (16-20).

In the third possible circumstance, the organization does poorly but the individual does very well. In this case, the high-performance individual is not in a position to expect the kind of organizational rewards listed in the first two circumstances. A mature management system should realize this. My best suggestion is that the same five performance levels above be recognized but that the pay scales be exactly half of what they normally would have been.

In the circumstance where the individual does poorly, it is my feeling that it doesn't make any difference what the organization did. The individual did not make the right kind of contribution and should not be rewarded. Rewarding for a poor performance is a guarantee to continue the same.

One complicating factor in this era of high inflation is what do you call a pay increase and what do you call an adjustment for inflation? I know of no organization that has completely solved that problem. In reality, even with the table above, this past year with inflation at 15 percent, if a top performer received 20 percent, in effect he is receiving only a net 5 percent reward for his performance. I believe the recommended pay percentages should be tied into the inflation rate. Theoretically, every organization should automatically modify its pay ranges based on the inflation level and then add the pay increase on top of inflation.

Bonus System

Working hand-in-hand with salary rewards based on individual achievement is the bonus system. This is nothing new of itself. But how does it work with MBO? If the organization meets certain understood, agreed-upon objectives and criteria, every organization member shares in the harvest. Objectives such as sales, profit, manufacturing efficiency, quality, and safety could be the bases. Criteria could be set for those deemed to be of importance based on the individual organization. The bonus system must be simple, straightforward, and understood.

The most important objective is profit. Good, solid, long-term-oriented profit is the golden word of capitalism. It's simple: no profit, no bonus. Other objectives can be a factor but only after profit objective is met.

The criterion for profit might be 15 percent before tax profit on sales. A pool is set up with 20 percent of all profit above the minimum criterion of 15 percent going into the pool. For example, a $40,000,000 sales company with $6,000,000 profit would have no bonuses. One company I am working with provides a nice working vacation at a popular resort area if the minimum criteria are met. Another idea would be to give some percentage such as 1 percent of all profits if the minimum criterion is met. However, a $7,000,000 profit would put $200,000 into a pool. If there were 500 employees, this would be a bonus of $400 per person. All employees share equally in this pool. The bonus is a nonbudgeted item.

Another way the pool can be distributed is to give divisional managers shares of the pool to distribute as they see fit within their units. This method is of doubtful value because of the bias problem. This is one instance in which I advocate treating everyone on the team the same. The bonus is the team reward. If the team wins the league championship, it goes to the Superbowl and everyone shares equally in the reward. If you don't win the league championship (in this case 15 percent profit before taxes) you stay home and everyone gets the same thing—nothing.

Under this system, a person has an opportunity to get ahead on his own and is also rewarded for being a team player.

I still believe the most effective way to handle a bonus is to include everyone, including the management team, by setting up a bonus fund. The fund is not budgeted, but comes out of after-tax corporate profits based on an audited financial statement. Another alternative is that funds should be available for bonus distribution unless the corporate performance exceeds all of the following: a) 10 percent return on sales before taxes, b) 5 percent return on sales after taxes, c) 80 percent manufacturing efficiency; and d) 40 percent sales growth increase. The total fund available for distribution each year is not to exceed 10 percent of corporate after-tax net profit or 1 percent of sales. This sets some standards, is reasonably simple, and lets everyone in on the bonus if things go well. Another criterion is 20 percent of after-tax profit in excess of 8 percent gross revenue.

Again, pay particular attention to the 20/80 rule. Those 20 percent who contribute the 80 percent need to be rewarded. A rigid reward system that holds them back just encourages them to go elsewhere. The other 80 percent are not going anywhere anyway so don't spend as much time worrying about them.

Incentives are finding a renewal. More and more organizations are looking at financial rewards. Despite the difficulties, incentives are growing in popularity. A survey of 2,000 companies conducted by Mercer Meidinger Hansen showed that 25 percent granted stock options or other incentives to middle- or lower-level employees who formerly were excluded from such plans. New participants most often got stock options, followed by annual incentives, usually in the form of one-time bonuses. Many of my clients are using a wide range of profit-sharing and other production/quality incentives.

Dr. Ken Matejka, in the Spring 1979 edition of the Arkansas Business Review, suggests the employee's rating of his boss. He lists 17 ways a person could rank his boss. His intention was to determine how people would feel about rating those items. After conferring with Dr. Matejka, we agreed a scale could be developed and the appraisal process would be a two-way street. The manager might need to have all the evaluations be done anonymously. A suggested form, Boss Evaluation, is provided below.

Next is provided a quick review of what has been covered. Examples of basketball, the situation I found at Continental Can in 1967, and a real estate business are given.

Boss Evaluation					
	Low/ Poor 1	Below Average 2	Average 3	Above Average 4	High/ Excellent 5
Depth of knowledge about work					
Awareness of recent developments in his field.					
Ability to help subordinates answer questions or solve problems.					
Ability to get people to accept ideas on what should be done.					
Willingness to adapt to new ideas and innovations.					
Ability to motivate subordinates.					
Interest in subordinates' welfare.					
Ability to provide an opportunity for subordinates to pursue their own ideas.					
Tolerance and respect for subordinates' opinions.					
Fairness and lack of personal prejudice.					
Attitude toward subordinates in terms of help, encouragement, advice, and friendliness.					
Ability to present oneself in a clear and organized manner,					
Interest and enthusiasm for job.					
Ability to communicate ideas and directives,					
Ability to listen well.					
Willingness to encourage two-way communication.					
Your overall opinion of him as a supervisor/manager.					
OVERALL MEAN					

	Basketball	1967-68 Continental Can	Real Estate Company
Purpose	Have prestigious, well-recognized, program	Survival and profit in the packaging business	Profit and survival in local ethical real estate business
Environmental Analysis	Statistics and analysis of other teams	Pork prices, trends in new packages	Housing starts up
Strengths and Weaknesses	Good shooters, weak bench,	Knowledgeable managers, poor organization	Experienced salesman new coach
Assumptions	Rules will stay the same	Demand for ham stays same. No governmental controls.	No labor strike
Objectives and Goals	Win NCAA by 1995, recruit 7-foot all-American high school player in 1991. Win 20 games 1991-92	Cut M.E. efficiency loss of - 17% by April 1968 to break even	Profit/sales of 10% in first quarter
Strategy	Have disciplined offense	Go after the fruit packers, government business	Heavy emphasis in southeast sections
Long-Range Plan	Schedule 15 teams in the top 10 over next 5 years	Relocate department in stages over next 5 years	Build new home office in southeast
Short-Range Plan	Visit high school of top 10 choices, visit parents, basketball camp in summer	Follow the MBO plan for the year and the budget	Ask for home-office bids in first quarter
Appraisal Recycling	22-6, recruiting questionable	Ran 10 straight weeks in black April 15, 1968	(See how you do each quarter)

Review, Checklist of Long-Range Planning/MBO

I.   Purpose

    A.   What is the reason for being for your mission, why needed, customers served, needs met in the marketplace, scope of the endeavor, nationwide, local, ethics, profit, nonprofit?

II.   Environmental Analysis

    A.   Pulse

    B.   Present of past

    C.   Industry surveys

    D.   Studies of future done now

III.   S&W (usually internal)

    A.   Human

    B.   Facilities/equipment

    C.   Patents/resources Natural

    D.   Financial

IV. Assumptions

    A.   You have no control over

    B.   Extend environmental analysis

    C.   Usually external

V. Objectives and Goals

    A.   Specific, time frame, measurable in key result areas. Note all rules for objectives.

VI. Strategy

    A.   Thinking stage

    B.   Where and how to commit resources

    C.   Timing

    D.   Pricing policy

VII. L.R.P.

    A.   Doing something in future

    B.   Build, hire, fire

    C.   Keep out results

    D.   Develop pro forma income/balance sheets

    E.   Sales forecast

    F.   Use action words

VIII. S.R.P.

    A.   What to do this year, this quarter

    B.   Oriented statements

    C.   First year of 5-year plan

    D.   Use action words

    E.   Zero-based budgeting

Assignment

Now, on a separate piece of paper, develop an in-depth long-range plan. Review the material presented and the notes you made at each subset. Use the checklist on the previous page to be sure you have each of the planning process stages set correctly.

Finish the book now for advice and discussion on the planning and MBO process.

References

Higgins, Richard B. "How Well Are We Rewarding Our Managers for Strategic Planning?" *Journal of Business Strategy*, 1(3) (Winter, 1981): 77.

Odiorne, George "MBO Special Report: Compensation: Thirty-Three Keys to Paying for Performance." Westfield, MS: MBO Press, 1976 (8 pages).

CHAPTER 12
CORPORATE CULTURE INDEX:
A BASE FOR STRATEGIC PLANNING AND MANAGEMENT

The culture of an organization is important to its life, contribution to society, and survival.

The opportunity to recognize and measure culture gives organization leaders the ability to understand and to better manage. A Corporate Culture Index has been developed.

The instrument to measure culture was given to businesses, hospitals, and churches. It was determined that a Corporate Culture Index could be developed for all those who participated.

What Is Corporate Culture?

A good definition of organizational culture was provided almost four decades ago by Elliott Jacques:

> "The customary or traditional ways of thinking and doing things, which are shared to a greater or lesser extent by all members of the organization and which new members must learn and at least partially accept in order to be accepted into the service of the firm."

The culture of an organization is generally viewed as a complete set of beliefs, ethics, values, ideologies, assumptions, and symbols. Culture is defined as the totality of socially transmitted behavior patterns, arts, beliefs, institutions, and all other products of human work and thought characteristic of a community or population. Another definition is basic and enduring values and beliefs which are widely held throughout the organization. These values and beliefs comprise the content of an organization's culture and are common understandings which are frequently taken for granted and which are reinforced by stories, symbols, rituals, and language systems. Intangible and unseen but known, these values and beliefs are distinguished from the concrete or visible manifestations of culture.

Most researchers conclude that corporate culture ascribes to the beliefs, principles, and behavior patterns that come together to shape the central individuality of each organization. Tulsa University professor, Donald D. Bowen, commented in a newspaper interview that corporate culture "includes a company's dress code, philosophy, public functions, communications, material goods, and physical environment."

Edgar Schein of Massachusetts Institute of Technology states that it is an incomplete notion that "culture is only a set of shared meanings that make it possible for members of a group to interpret and act upon their environment."

A culture is a template of basic assumptions that a particular group has invented, discovered, or devised in learning to deal with its problems of external adaption and internal integration. This template has worked well enough to be considered valid, therefore it is taught to new individuals in the organization as the correct way to think, feel, and perceive in accordance with other problems.

The corporate culture of an organization can be analyzed at many different levels. The visible artifacts or the developed environment of the company are its manner of visible or audible behavior patterns, unspoken doctrine, architecture, technological level or current modernity, employee orientation, materials, public documents, characters, credo statements, or even books of discipline. This level of cultural analysis is difficult data to evaluate because it is easy to find and difficult to interpret. Descriptions can be given on how behavior patterns are discernible among the members, but it is common not to be able to know the true reason why the organization acts the way it does.

Typically speaking, all organizations have some set of values that guide their behavior (second box in 12-1). As a result of the elusive nature of an innate value system, it is difficult to observe values directly. This forces organizations to research their character documents, doctrines or interview key personnel to glean any concrete information. The problem with this value information is that it is only a personal perception of why they behave the way they do, rather than the true motivation which is generally cloaked or unconscious.

To get to the root of culture, this concealed or unconscious motivation behind the outward behavior must be discovered. These learned values are forces behind the decision-making process. The decision made is based on an assumption which is soon frequently forgotten. Assumptions which are taken for granted are very powerful, ingrained characteristics. Power renders assumptions less debatable or adjustable than given values. Some examples of such assumptions would be, that schools should educate, businesses should be profitable, medicine should prolong life, and churches should be religious. These are assumptions even though they are often considered values.

Controlling values can be divided into: (1) ultimate, non-debatable, taken-for-granted values, for which the term assumptions is more appropriate, and (2) debatable, overtly espoused values for which the term values is more applicable (see Chart 12-1).

There are different positions taken on the cohesiveness of organizational culture. Many scholars believe that a strong culture with a well-defined set of guiding beliefs is better than a weak culture that has less of a bonding nature. Not only do individual businesses have strong cultures, but links among business, the banking industry, and the government are also cultural and very powerful. Japan, Inc., is actually an expansion of the corporate culture idea on a national scale.

Chart 12-1
The Levels of Culture and their Interaction

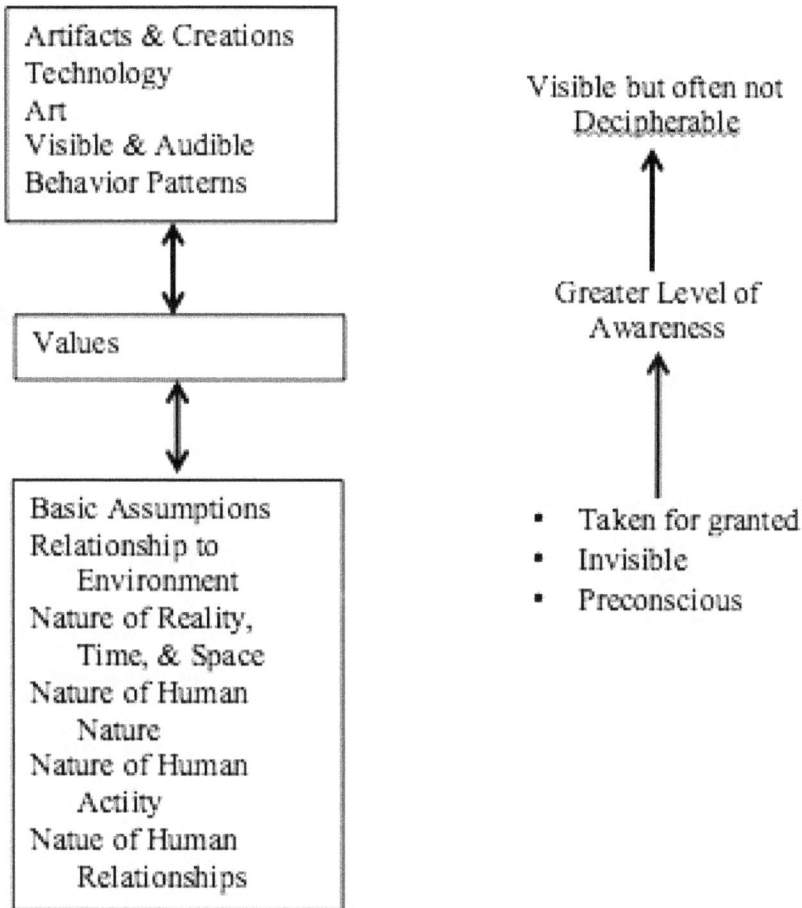

Artifacts & Creations Technology Art Visible & Audible Behavior Patterns	Visible but often not Decipherable

↕

Values	Greater Level of Awareness

↕

Basic Assumptions Relationship to 　Environment Nature of Reality, 　Time, & Space Nature of Human 　Nature Nature of Human 　Actiity Natue of Human 　Relationships	• Taken for granted • Invisible • Preconscious

Organizations have ingrained cultures. It is believed that a strong culture denotes agreement among the members of the organization. Also, strong culture promotes cohesion of all those who wish to be an active part of the organizational structure or membership body. The extent of the bond and harmony that remains among the values and ideologies, is a measure of the internal fit or attachment that characterizes the culture. Chart 12-2 shows the different factors in the organization in relation to the main objective of performance. Failing to practice consistency within the structure can provide a degree of incompatibility among individual groups with regard to the values of the espoused culture.

A survey of chief executive officers revealed that most believed that organizational cultures are real, and that strong cultures contribute to corporate success. Forty percent said they believed strongly enough to try to deal with culture in a serious manner.

Chart 12-2
Cultural Influence

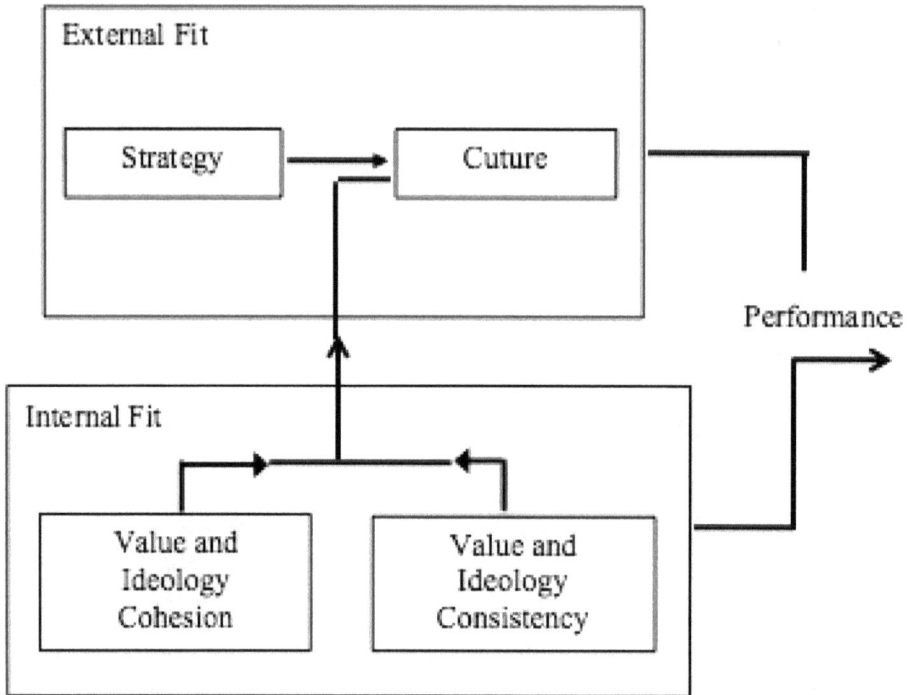

Development of Corporate Culture Index

An index is developed to measure corporate culture. By definition, it is illusive at best with every organization being unique and having a culture all its own. After working with a wide range of public and private companies, (government related, nonprofit and ministry/church related), the differences can be quickly detected.

A basic assumption when developing an index is that you know what to measure and how much weight to put on each factor involved. For research purposes and this paper, the following categories were determined as important in measuring the culture in an organization:

1.	Goals	11.	Values
2.	Planning	12.	Training
3.	Planning Effectiveness	13.	Unique
4.	Morale	14.	Social
5.	Performance Appraisals	15.	Ethics
6.	Rewards	16.	Leader
7.	Freedom	17.	Interaction
8.	Communication	18.	Benefits
9.	Job Satisfaction	19.	Perception
10.	People	20.	Environment

The measurement method is designed to create a negative and positive opportunity for each category. If the culture is very favorable, it will have a higher positive score. If poor culture, it will be a lower score. The index is the combined measurement of the positive minus the negative scores.

No attempt is made to determine if upper management is satisfied with its culture index. It is beyond the scope of this paper to suggest that culture affects the bottom line in key result areas. In contrast, the Strategic Planning Institute's PIMS model suggests, for example, that market share has the largest impact on normal profit. There is no proof today that culture directly affects normal profit, although opinions might suggest it does.

It can be seen that the total Corporate Culture Index score (CCI) is close in regard to a possible high of 100 or low of 20. Company Two scores the highest with a score of 61.3. Figure 2, Ministry One, is next, with a score of 57.9, and Company One, follows with a score of 54.5. (See Figure 1 and Figure 3.) A closer examination of the 20 categories is needed to provide more information as to how the organization has performed in comparison with others. An example of this could be shown in the area of planning effectiveness of Company One and Ministry One with scores of 1.6 and 1.7 respectively, contrasted with Company Two's score of 3.0. This can even be further broken down on the MSBS score (also part of total CCI questionnaire): Company One, Ministry One, and Company Two are -0.76, -0.80, and .43, respectively. The scope value is incidental in these cases, the performance among them is what is important. An understanding of what these scores mean is made intelligible by evaluating the questionnaire. (A sample is in Appendix B. Figure 4 on pages 19 and 20 give sample questions asked into the 20 different areas.) Planning effectiveness (question three) is section IX(a-d), IX£, and IX g. Question IX, a, for example, specifically deals with the strategic plan being followed. It gives more opportunity for personal recognition: (1) not at all, (2) slightly, (3) moderately, (4) considerably, and (5) very much so. Has the employee had the opportunity to satisfy his higher level needs? This specific example of planning effectiveness is segmented in possible response scores. As noted, rankings one through five give a value to the particular area investigated. When compiled, the other 19 areas are formulated in a similar fashion of questions and valued responses to create the possible CCI score of 100. Pursuing these inner drives and motivations is necessary to understand the employees' fulfillment. Performance is always the concern of the task-oriented organization, to understand and utilize the most from the staff that really wants to be part of the team.

As additional information becomes available, the telltale sign of performance on the CCI score will provide an index of possible achievement. This, in comparison with other businesses, profit or nonprofit, of the same nature, can be evaluated on how they are progressing internally. The staff of the organization then can understand that perhaps they are, nationally speaking, doing well, but that there are weak areas that need improvement, or that nationally their performance is below par in most areas, and this signifies the need for change.

The next task is to develop an index with a large data base to provide organizations with enough information to accurately assess where they are and where they could be within their own given situation.

Conclusion

It is important to identify and measure the culture of an organization. A culture index has been developed so that each participating organization can measure its culture against others. In each of the 20 categories, each organization can make comparisons. Especially important at this time is how the organization is perceived by the outside community. Scores in these categories indicate a need for serious self-examination followed by planned public relations plans on how to bolster that negative image. Low scores on how the organization is being managed, and high turnover of employees dictate a need to look at how the planning and management system operate. Closer examination of an organization's culture could assist it to adapt and be more effective.

A total of 30 organizations were tested. The Management System Balance Sheet and Corporate Culture Index were calculated for each organization. Top management was presented the data in each case. The conclusion was that the

MSBS and CCI did, in fact, measure perceptions of how the organization was managed and give an accurate measure of culture.

A consultant with McKinsey and Company has stated that to manage successfully, a company must (1) decide what kind of culture is needed in the organization, (2) evaluate the existing culture to determine where gaps exist between the actual and desired cultures, (3) decide how to close these gaps, and (4) repeat the entire process periodically. The CI as developed gives managers the four options. The management team could determine what the score in each of the 20 categories should be. They could evaluate where they are with the CI. Then an action plan could be developed to close the gap. Both the MSBS and CI can be measured periodically to keep culture where it should be.

Blake and Mouton state that Corporate Culture is "the attitudes, beliefs, and values of its people along with traditions, precedents, and past practices of the organization comprise that organization's culture, its way of doing business. It may be integrated around values of achievement and excellence, woven around seniority and benefits, or may reveal disinterest, apathy, and hopelessness. It significantly influences how people apply or withhold their energies. To attempt to change a firm which is ineffective or marginally effective into a highly effective one despite its culture, at the worst is likely to be futile and at the best, of limited success. It may even generate stronger negative attitudes and deeper resistances and produce a worse corporate performance than formerly existed."

Blake and Mouton believe that culture does have an effect on how the organization is managed. They say corporate culture results in organizational work which is:

Completely Sound: attitudes, values, and beliefs, and traditions, precedents, and practices which currently influence corporate members have the effect of stimulating efforts to produce, achieve, and accomplish. Excellence is a value throughout the corporation, and it has a strong and constructive impact on short term operations and long term planning.

Almost Completely Sound, *Quite Sound*

Moderately Sound

As Sound As Unsound, which means: corporate culture contains some positive elements which promote productive effort and accomplishment, but others which restrict people from applying their energies so as to further excellence, tradition, the company way, and how things were done in the past tend to stifle approaches based upon actualities, status quoism is a key to understanding attitudes, efforts, and actions.

Moderately Unsound, *Quite Unsound*

Almost Completely Unsound

Completely Unsound, which means: traditions, precedents, and practices, expectations, beliefs, and values bear little relationship to productive achievement or profit seeking, apathy and indifference are in the warp and woof of the culture, militant resistance and antagonism toward the corporation are evident.

Using the Culture Index, the CI provides a measure to monitor and improve performance. Last year at my annual physical exam, my blood pressure was 160/100. That was a measure of a present condition. I had to develop objectives and strategy to improve an unfavorable score. A few months ago at this years physical, the blood pressure was 120/80. Why the improvement? I knew the score and took action. A number of organizations use the CI to monitor the planning, management and control system.

SUMMARY OF M.S.B.S. - COMPANY ONE

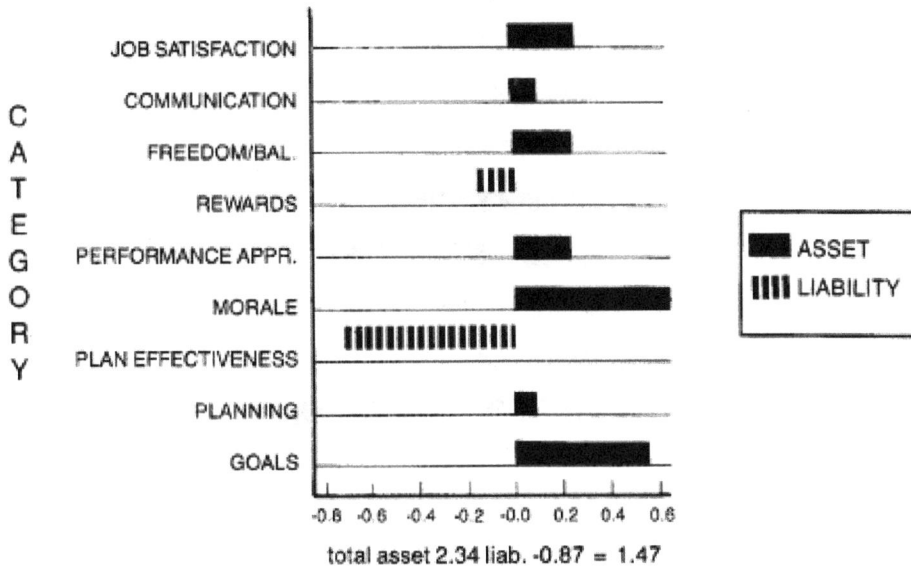

total asset 2.34 liab. -0.87 = 1.47

SUMMARY OF C.C.I. - COMPANY ONE

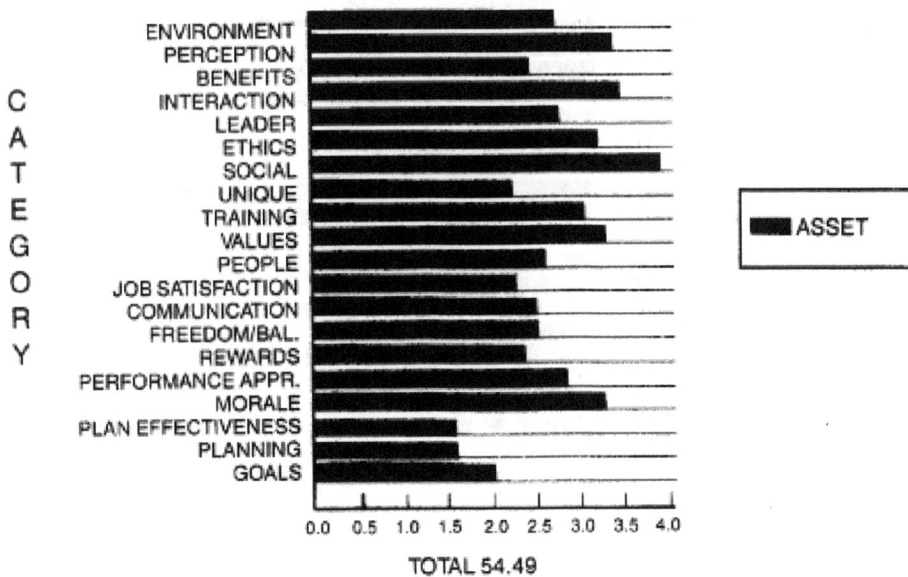

TOTAL 54.49

SUMMARY OF M.S.B.S. - COMPANY TWO

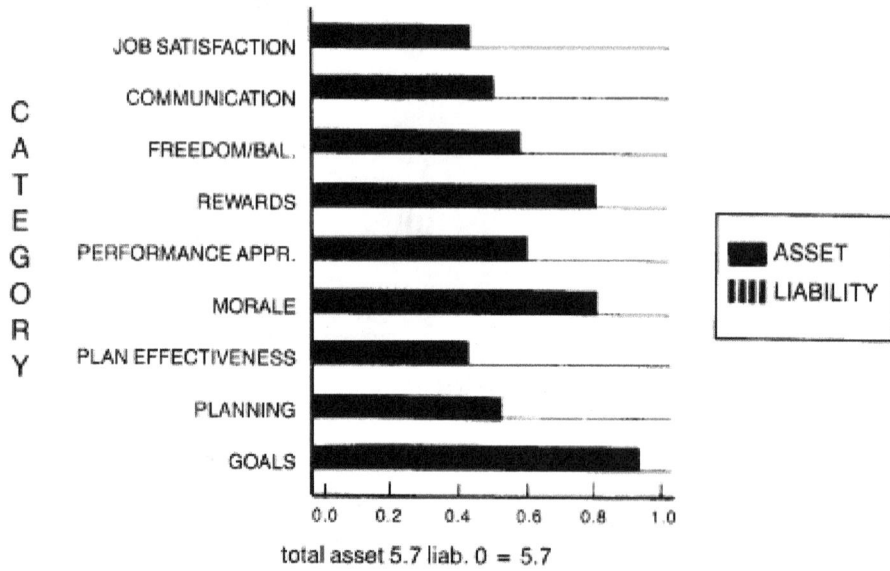

total asset 5.7 liab. 0 = 5.7

SUMMARY OF C.C.I. - COMPANY TWO

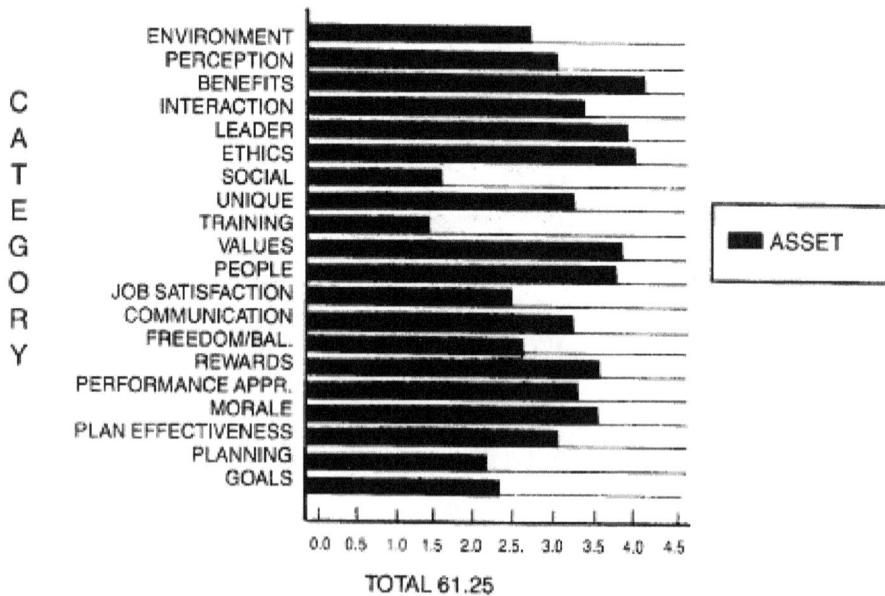

TOTAL 61.25

SUMMARY OF M.S.B.S. - MINISTRY ONE

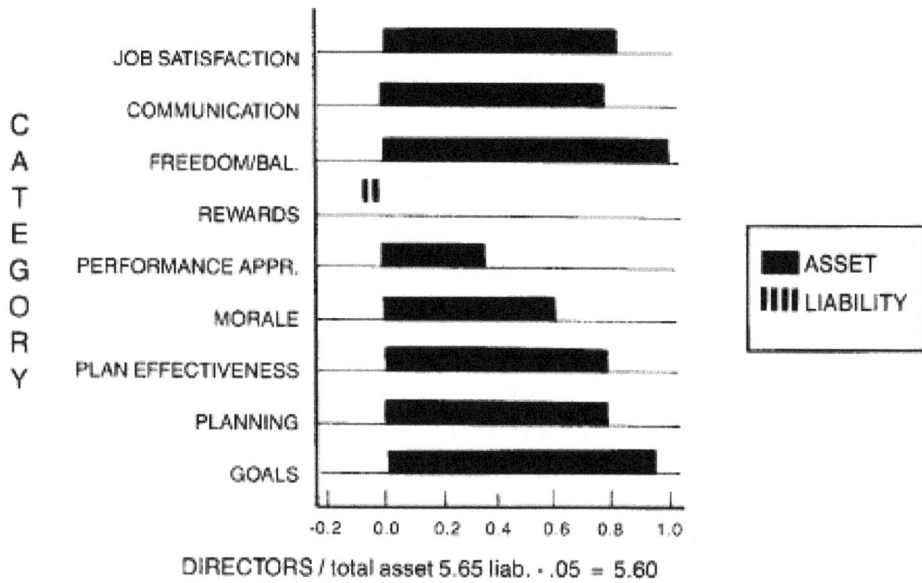

DIRECTORS / total asset 5.65 liab. - .05 = 5.60

SUMMARY OF C.C.I. - MINISTRY ONE

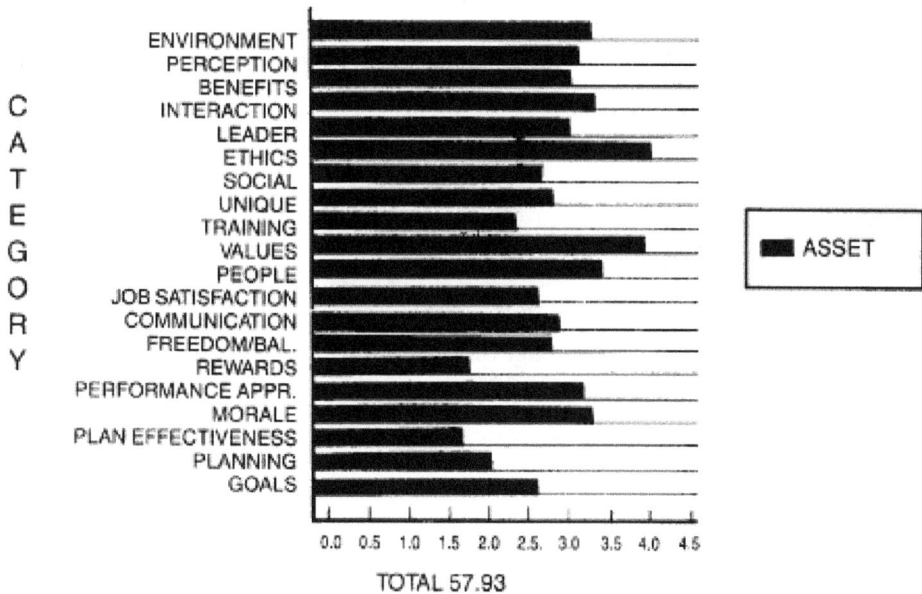

TOTAL 57.93

References

Arogyaswany, Bernard and Byles, Charles M., "Organizational Culture: Internal and External Fits" *Journal of Management,* 13(4), 1987: 647-658.

Baker, Edwin L., "Managing Organizational Culture" *Management Review,* July 1980:8-13.

Bowen, Donald D., "A Company's Culture Can Affect Its Performance" Tulsa, OK: *Tulsa Business Chronicle.*

Byles, Charles M. and Keating, Robert J., *Strength of Organizational Culture and Performance: Strategic Implications* Stillwater, OK: Oklahoma State University.

Dean, T. E. and A. A. Kennedy. *Corporate Cultures: The Rites and Rituals of Corporate Life* Reading, MA: Addison-Wesley, 1982.

Denison, Daniel R. *The Climate Culture and Effectiveness of Work Organizations: A Study of Organizational Behavior and Financial Performance,* Ann Arbor, MI: University of Michigan, 1982.

Gardner, M., "Creating A Corporate Culture for the Eighties" *Business Horizons,* January/February 1985:59-63. For some of the problems involved in creating a culture, see A. L. Wilkins and N. J. Bristow, "For Successful Organizational Culture, Honor Your Past" *Academy of Management Executive, August.* 1987:221-229.

Jacques, Elliott, *The Changing Culture of a Factory.* London: Tavistock Institute 1951:251.

Migliore, Henry R., and Neal Bratschun, *Using Management System Balance Sheets,* March/April, 1987.

"Paradise, Corporate Style" *Business Month,* July/August 1988: 47.

Schein, Edgar H., *Coming To a New Awareness of Organizational Culture,* Massachusetts Institute of Technology. *Sloan Management Review,* Winter 1984.

The New American Heritage Dictionary of The English Language Boston, MA: Houghton Mifflin Company, 1978:321.

Wright, J. P., *On a Clear Day You Can See General Motors,* Gross Point, MI: Wright Enterprises, 1979:149.

CHAPTER 13
CONCLUSIONS AND RECOMMENDATIONS

This book has told the story of the successful application of a system of management. I chose the title Strategic Long-Range Planning/MBO to describe this philosophy. You can see that this description is greatly expanded beyond the traditional definition. I feel strongly that this philosophy must include many steps before objectives are set. The key word then becomes management through the use of objectives in an orderly long-range planning system.

I stood with a consulting friend at a long-drawn-out social gathering. An acquaintance introduced his wife and she shared about her new job with a new business being started in Tulsa. With nothing else to talk about, we discussed the things that would guarantee failure. The list included: *don't* do a feasibility study to see if another station was needed, *don't* develop a strategic plan, *don't* ask advice from anyone, go on the air immediately, *don't* develop a marketing plan, hire salespersons with no defined criteria, *don't* have a target market, forget any kind of market research to find out the listening preference, *don't* analyze the competition. Someone must have heard our conversation because all these things were done. The company has been a lost cause from the start.

As we know, 50 percent of small businesses fail the first year and 80 percent by year five. I am continually baffled at how many businesses/churches/organizations are started this way. I have managed successfully using objectives since 1964. From those days in manufacturing on the third shift with Continental Can Company to its present use with scores of clients. Students have learned my brand of Long-Range Planning/MBO and have used it in a wide range of occupations. They report successful experiences ranging from a chaplaincy in the Navy to management of a food service, proving that this philosophy can be learned and used by others. I sincerely hope that this book will help management deal successfully with its most important resource: people.

This book has attempted to make the following points:

1. There is a systematic, logical way to develop a long-range plan.

2. MBO has evolved into a long-range strategic planning system.

3. Everyone can be and should be involved in the planning process.

4. We do have a productivity problem in the United States.

5. Many organizations have had successful experiences with MBO.

6. Some organizations have had unsuccessful experiences, however.

7. Unsuccessful applications can be traced to a few well-defined causes.

8. MBO is more successful as a system of management when it is implemented from the top down rather than by a staff function such as personnel.

9. Planning and a management style based on person-oriented theory are derivatives of successful MBO applications.

10. MBO is applicable at the lowest levels of the organization.

11. The theoretical contributions from most academic scholars support MBO theory.

12. Commitment and self-control are the keys to MBO success.

13. There is a proper way to write meaningful objectives.

14. The perceived extent and effectiveness of MBO can be quantified.

15. I have successfully implemented the Long-Range Planning/MBO philosophy discussed in this book in the following settings: railroad, coal mine, oil company, church, government, and education.

My experience with and study of this brand of management and MBO led me to make these observations:

1. MBO is not a current fad but has evolved with our country's industrialization.

2. MBO is not a staff program, but rather a top-to-bottom philosophy of management.

3. Every organization and each decentralized entity within an organization should adapt MBO to its own needs.

4. Goals must be negotiated to as high a degree as possible.

5. Periodic reviews are a must.

6. Both extrinsic and intrinsic rewards must be obtainable to as high a degree as possible for the individual and/or the group he works in.

7. There are methods for setting, reviewing, and updating MBO that require minimum paperwork.

8. Organizations must use consultants who have insight into the fundamentals of MBO, not merely a preconceived format.

9. MBO has applicability from top levels right down to the blue- and white-collar levels.

10. If you start using MBO, begin benefiting from its use, and then stop, a big drop off in morale will result.

11. We have a problem in equating objective attainment with extrinsic rewards.

There is an indication that MBO is not perceived to be doing enough in the area of measurement of performance and rewards. It would appear that if MBO is to have a long-term effect, providing a positive motivational climate, a fair and concise means of measuring and rewarding performance must be used. I suspect, based on observations over the last decade, that the major problem to be overcome is that of tying the extrinsic rewards pay, bonuses, and so forth, to performance. This program area offers the opportunity for research to gain more insight into the problem.

Recommendations

An organization thinking about instituting a long-range planning/MBO program should consider the following points:

1. The decision to implement this management philosophy should not be made in haste.

2. To the extent possible, it should receive management support.

3. It is strongly recommended that some type of training session take place in a neutral environment.

4. An outside resource person is needed to get the program started.

5. A person from the organization should be assigned to work with the consultant so that he can take over as the in-house expert.

6. Each organization must find the best way for its people to set objectives.

7. Each organization should come up with its own best method for handling feedback and reviews.

8. Be prepared to expose your management team to new ideas and new ways of approaching managerial problems.

9. Ways should be found to involve all employees in some decision making.

10. Performance reviews must be conducted at regular, scheduled intervals.

11. Be prepared to spend time and hard work keeping the program viable, especially in the first six months.

12. Every organization and each decentralized entity in a decentralized organization can adapt MBO to its organization.

13. Goals must be negotiated to as high a degree as possible, rather than imposed unilaterally by management.

14. Periodic reviews are a must, and must be done by the boss.

15. Both extrinsic and intrinsic rewards must be obtainable to as high a degree as possible for the individual and the group he works in.

16. Use methods for setting, reviewing, and updating MBO that require minimum paperwork.

17. Don't let a staff department dominate your program.

18. Set up a schedule and timetable for strategic planning.

One of the most important features of this Strategic Planning Process is that the top-management team agree on a strategic plan which, by its very nature, establishes the overall direction for the organization. Because of this involvement by all members of the management team, a consensus is reached through study and compromise.

Another important requirement is that the organization subunits then go through the very same process and get the same result, the same kind of involvement and consensus out of its organization members.

Still another important requirement is that the chain reaction of involvement go down into the organization all the way to its lowest levels. Theoretically, the process of identifying the targets and objectives, responsibilities, and follow-up needed go right down to the janitor. The net effect of this planning system is that everyone in the organization is tied to the overall purpose and plan. The system of feedback and review makes everyone aware of what is going on and serves as a scorecard of the organization's progress toward its goals. The individual organization members have an opportunity to satisfy their higher-level needs for involvement, recognition, and individual development. Once a person sees that his personal goals are being met, both the intrinsic and extrinsic rewards, he is tied more closely to the organization's goals. The result is a chain reaction with the organization being able to adapt to changing times, objectives being met, persons tied to the organization, their needs being met, and a good, healthy organization serving the needs of everyone involved.

At the root of this Strategic Planning System is the fact that the top corporate team and the highest levels set the organization's direction. The firm is not driven by the marketing plan, finance plan, or perhaps the production plan as is often the case in many organizations. Marketing, production, and finance develop their plans after the overall plan is set. Marketing does the normal forecasting, situation analysis, product development, and other things that go into a strategic plan. A recent book by Dr. Robert Stevens discusses how a strategic marketing plan fits in with the overall company plan.

The financial plan must have projections of income statements, balance sheets, and cash budgets to show how the organization will progress financially through the time period of the plan. The manufacturing plan, similarly, must be geared to producing products called for in the marketing plan, intricately interwoven with the financial plan to be able to update capital equipment needed and interacting with the people plan to be sure that organization members are there to ensure production of the plan.

The people plan then must take into account all the needs of the people to manage the organization. It must concern itself with factors all the way from executive compensation, bonus plans, retirement, insurance policies and procedures, down to scheduling vacations.

At this point, it is well to mention budgets. Strategic plans should be the central managing entity of organizations, with the budget being the allocation and review arm that ensures execution of the strategic plan.

Capital budgets can be approved within dollar limits over the five-year scope of the strategic plan, with the normal capital budgeting approval procedure used to justify individual projects within that overall approved capital budget.

Of critical importance is the timing of the steps in the strategic planning process. The following sequence is being used by a number of organizations and has proved successful.

Note there is a constant overlap. By July, top management is already projecting another year into the future and dropping the current year in the five-year strategic plan.

This does not mean they are not conscious of the current year, they are, and must manage, control, and make key decisions to finish out the current year. What top management is doing is constantly pushing the planning horizon, looking through the clouds, and providing direction for the organization in an organized manner.

Although this sequence of events seems rigid, it puts the organization in a position to make fast, logical decisions. All members of management are familiar with the approved strategic plan. When new opportunities present themselves or a crisis appears, the organization must be in a position to react quickly. The strategic plan is the focal point of this reaction.

For example, during the oil embargo crisis in 1974, I was interviewing one of Frontier Airlines' middle managers on how he used MBO. A phone call came in from his boss at the corporate office. During the next hour the manager I was interviewing completely renegotiated the plan and objectives for his responsibility area. An environmental factor, the oil embargo, affected the operation of the company. An assumption that there would be adequate fuel to run the airline had to be changed. Top management of Frontier made new plans and started renegotiating plans with the next level down. A subtle but important thing happened. The man I was interviewing had complete input into how plans, schedules and operations would be changed in his responsibility areas. He was in on the decisions and when the conference call was completed, was set to react immediately with enthusiasm. I stayed the rest of the day watching a top-level manager use MBO to perfection. Everyone down to the people selling tickets knew the new game plan in a matter of hours.

The key ability to react was the strategic plan. On both ends of the phone were Frontier executives looking at the same plan and literally making changes and agreeing on them with notations on their plans. The discussions were confirmed with memos.

How many times have we seen organizations meet a critical crossroad where a few managers make a decision and say let's go this way, and throw the entire organization into chaos? The organization does not know how to react, where to go, or what to do. Everyone is second-guessing the decisions. The organization then slowly reacts to the new changes.

The strategic planning/MBO system outlined in this book creates a management climate to react to change. I have every reason to believe that the strategic planning process discussed in this book will work in every kind of profit and nonprofit organization. To date, I have assisted more than 500 organizations in using the Strategic Planning and Management Process.

As we enter the 21st Century there are great opportunities for the business firm. Many will prosper. Not all will survive into the 22nd Century. The principles and philosophy of this book can contribute to the success and survival of the organization.

R. HENRY MIGLIORE, PhD, is a leading strategist for long-term planning for business, sports, and religious leaders. He offers consulting services as well as resources including books, videos, articles, seminars, and training sessions.

He is currently the president of Managing for Success, an international consulting company. Dr. Migliore teaches at the graduate and undergraduate levels at universities worldwide. He was Professor of Management and former Dean of the ORU School of Business from 1975 until 1987. From 1887 to 2003 he was Facet Enterprises Professor of Management at UCT/'NSU Tulsa. From 2003 to date he has worked worldwide as author, visiting professor and consultant. He is currently assisting ORU Global Outreach Center with broadcasts to various target markets worldwide.

He is a former manager of the press manufacturing operations of the Continental Can Company's Stockyard Plant. Prior to that he was responsible for the industrial engineering function at Continental's Indiana plant. In this capacity, Dr. Migliore was responsible for coordinating the long-range planning process. In addition, he has had various consulting experiences with Fred Rudge & Associates in New York and has served large and small businesses, associations, and non-profit organizations in various capacities.

He has made presentations to a wide variety of clubs, groups, and professional associations. Dr. Migliore has been selected to be on the faculty for the International Conferences on Management by Objectives and Strategic Planning Institute Seminar Series and he is a frequent contributor to the Academy of Management. He served for 12 years on the Board of Directors of T.D. Williamson, Inc., and was previously on the Boards of the International MBO Institute and Brush Creek Ranch, American Red Cross/Tulsa Chapter, and is chairman of a scholarship fund for Eastern State College. In 1984, he was elected into the Eastern State College Athletic Hall of Fame. Dr. Migliore has been a guest lecturer on a number of college campuses, including Harvard, Texas A&M, Pepperdine, ITESM, Guadalajara, Autonoma De Guadalajara, and University of Calgary Executive Development programs. He serves on many chamber and civic committees. He was selected Who's Who on a list of 31 top echelon writers and consultants in America.

Dr. Migliore's books have been translated into Russian, Chinese, Korean, Spanish, German, and Japanese.

He has 17 books in total. His next book in process is *Fourth Quarter Redefined*.

HENRY MIGLIORE
4ᵀᴴ QUARTER REDEFINED
THE LEGACY CONTINUES

R. HENRY MIGLIORE, PhD

PRESIDENT OF MANAGING FOR SUCCESS

10839 SOUTH HOUSTON • JENKS, OK 74037 • (918) 299-0007

EMAIL: HMIGLIORE@AOL.COM
WEBSITE: WWW.HMIGLIORE.COM • YOUTUBE: DRMIGLIORE

www.ingramcontent.com/pod-product-compliance
Lightning Source LLC
Chambersburg PA
CBHW061754210326
41518CB00036B/2363